# Hidden Treasures

**'Even in darkness light dawns for the upright ...'**
Psalm 112:4

## Selwyn Hughes
Revised and updated by Mick Brooks
**FURTHER STUDY: IAN SEWTER**

© CWR 2012. Dated text previously published as *Every Day with Jesus: Treasures of Darkness* (Nov/Dec 1990) by CWR. This edition revised and updated for 2012 by Mick Brooks.

CWR, Waverley Abbey House, Waverley Lane, Farnham, Surrey GU9 8EP, UK
**Tel: 01252 784700** Email: mail@cwr.org.uk
Registered Charity No. 294387. Registered Limited Company No. 1990308.

Unless otherwise stated, all Scripture quotations are from the Holy Bible, New International Version. © International Bible Society.

Cover image: Getty/Stockbyte/Steven Nourse.
Quiet Time image: sxc.hu/kavitha
Printed in England by Linney Print

MIX
Paper from
responsible sources
FSC® C015900

*Every Day with Jesus* is available in large print from CWR. It is also available on audio and DAISY in the UK and Eire for the sole use of those with a visual impairment worse than N12, or who are registered blind. For details please contact **Torch Trust for the Blind**, Tel: 01858 438260. Torch Trust for the Blind, Torch House, Torch Way, Northampton Road, Market Harborough, LE16 9HL.

# A word of introduction ...

It hardly seems possible that we have reached the final months of 2012. This year has been an eventful one to say the least. CWR has seen God at work in new and exciting ways. The UK has been gripped with Olympic fever, and the Queen's Diamond Jubilee has been celebrated. We have witnessed the highs and lows of the Eurozone Crisis, the Double Dip Recession and the European Football Championship. And then there are our personal tragedies and triumphs.

In this issue, Selwyn gets to grips with the truth that whatever our circumstances, there is, with God, treasure to be found. As Ralph Waldo Emerson once said, 'This time, like all times, is a very good one, if we but know what to do with it.'

Drawing on his long experience as a disciple of Jesus, teacher and counsellor, Selwyn provides a map to guide us towards God's richest blessings along the way. And even when we find ourselves walking a dark path, we find that it isn't a dead end. Scott Peck, a popular author and psychiatrist, observed, 'Our finest moments are most likely to occur when we are feeling deeply uncomfortable, unhappy and unfulfilled. For it is only in such moments, propelled by our discomfort, that we are likely to step out of our ruts and start searching for different ways and for truer answers'.

So, we end this year with Selwyn's encouragement that whether faced with clear blue skies or the fog of confusion, we can come to know God in a way we never knew Him before.

Sincerely yours, in His name

Mick

Mick Brooks, Consulting Editor

---

 Free small-group resources to accompany this issue can be found at www.cwr.org.uk/extra and you can now join the *EDWJ* conversation on Facebook www.facebook.com/edwjpage

# Hidden treasures

## FOR READING & MEDITATION - ISAIAH 45:1-17

'I will give you the treasures of darkness ... so that you may know
that I am the LORD ...' (v.3)

As the year draws to a close, we consider the theme: *Hidden Treasures*. Those who regularly follow these Bible notes will know that it is my custom to approach every issue from a different angle. Sometimes I focus on a book or passage, and thus the approach is analytical and expositional. Sometimes the purpose is functional and practical, exploring spiritual growth and how to live well as a follower of Jesus. And on occasions (such as this), the approach is devotional and inspirational – portraying biblical truths that are designed to warm the heart and set fire to the soul. In this way, a varied spiritual menu is presented – a method necessary not only to assist spiritual growth but to satisfy the wide tastes of an ever-growing readership.

The devotional theme I have chosen for this closing issue of the year, brims over with hope and confidence – a hope and a confidence that are much needed, for many times we find ourselves walking in darkness. Perhaps you are there at this moment. Our understanding of why God chooses to lead us into the darkness is revealed to us in our text for today, 'I will give you the *treasures* of darkness' (my emphasis).

**FURTHER STUDY**

Prov. 25:2;
Col. 2:1-10

1. Why does God conceal treasures in darkness?

2. Where is treasure hidden?

Are there treasures which can only be found in the dark? It would seem so. John Bunyan found them in the darkness of prison and wrote the immortal story, *Pilgrim's Progress*. Helen Keller, blind and deaf and dumb, found treasures in her darkness and shared them with the world through her glowing spirit. In a deep dark well you can look up and see the stars, even when people in the light above can't see them. We can discover treasures in the darkness that we would never be able to find in the light.

**O Father, help me learn the secret of turning all my periods of darkness into occasions of delight - delight at the discovery of Your hidden treasures. In Jesus' name I ask it. Amen.**

# 'Next summer's apples ...'

**FOR READING & MEDITATION - HEBREWS 5:1-14**
'Although he was a son, he learned obedience from
what he suffered ...' (v.8)

Yesterday we raised the question: are there treasures which can only be found in the dark? Yes, it would seem so, we said, for history is replete with illustrations of how people made discoveries in the darkness that they might not have made in the light. A Christian woman woke up one morning in the dead of winter with the words ringing in her mind, 'Next summer's apples are already on the tree.' How strange, she thought, for as she looked out through her window, she saw nothing but snow and ice. Then the Spirit said, 'You may not see the apples yet, but they are there, nevertheless. And in the same way, the treasures of summer are already in the tree of life, caught at this moment in the darkness of the winter's cold. Be patient, for love will soon bring them out.'

**FURTHER STUDY**

Rom. 5:1-5;
Heb. 10:32-39

1. What does suffering produce?

2. Why can we joyfully accept suffering?

I have chosen the verse for today '... he learned trusting-obedience by what he suffered ...' (*The Message*), because it emphasises the point I want to make throughout this issue, namely, that the place of darkness can be the place of delight. Jesus, we are told, *learned* by all He suffered. How strange that the Son of God should learn anything. Did He not have all knowledge and wisdom? Yes He did, but when He took upon Himself our flesh He deliberately and voluntarily limited Himself to finding out about life in the way we find out – by grappling with issues day after day. He learned that 'treasure' in 'darkness' – the darkness of suffering.

Milton found great treasures in the darkness of his blindness and revealed them to the world in verse. Sometimes a *dark* tunnel is the shortest way around a hill.

**Father, help me to remember that no matter how dark and cold the winter, the treasures of summer are already in the tree. Etch this truth so deeply into my spirit that it will never fade. In Christ's name I pray. Amen.**

# Dig for meaning

### FOR READING & MEDITATION - PSALM 18:16-30

'You, O Lord, keep my lamp burning; my God turns my darkness into light.' (v.28)

**T**oday we ask: what must we do when we find ourselves surrounded by darkness? We must look for the *meaning* that lies within it. Whenever you find yourself engulfed in darkness, begin to dig by the light of your flickering torch of faith for the treasures of meaning that are hidden there. For be assured of this: the treasures of darkness are found by those who look for meaning. I have known many Christians who have allowed the darkness to drag their spirits down to such a degree that they have lost their faith. They did not know how to search out the treasures that lay all around them.

Paul must have inwardly chafed when he found himself in the darkness of a prison cell – confined for no other crime than that of announcing the good news. The curtailment of his personal liberty was hard, but it was harder still to be shut off from the opportunity of telling men and women about his beloved Saviour. What could compensate for that? But in the darkness he found a treasure. Paul's letters, mostly written from prison, have enriched Christians down the centuries and will continue to do so, until Jesus comes again. They could not have been written except in the darkness of a prison experience. Paul dipped his pen in the blood of his sufferings and wrote words that are deathless. In long days and nights of pondering upon Jesus, his thoughts crystallised into immortal phrases through which men and women have looked into the heart of a redeeming God.

One thing is sure – God will never allow us to be surrounded by darkness without handing us a pick so that we can dig for treasure.

### FURTHER STUDY

Job 28:1-10;
Matt. 13:44-45;
Acts 17:10-12

1. How do we obtain treasures in darkness?

2. How did the Bereans dig for meaning?

**Father, I see that the treasures of darkness come only to those who dig for meaning. Help me not to rebel against the darkness but rejoice in it – because with Your help I can turn the place of darkness into the place of discovery. Amen.**

# Having the right attitude

**FOR READING & MEDITATION - ROMANS 8:28-39**
'If God is for us, who can be against us?' (v.31)

**W**e are seeing that when we are engulfed in darkness, that is the time to light the flickering torch of faith and explore the treasures that are hidden there. The very first thing we need to understand when we are surrounded by deep darkness is that we are not going to be exempt from the difficult periods of life just because we are Christians. If we react to dark experiences by saying, 'I'm a Christian, why is this happening to me?' then this will hinder us from finding the treasures that lie all around. Richard Baxter wrote concerning the Great Plague: 'At first so few of the religious people were taken away that they began to get puffed up and boast of the great differences which God did make. But quickly after that, they all fell alike.'

**FURTHER STUDY**

Job 42:1-13;
Luke 22:39-42

1. What was the result of Job's suffering?

2. What was Christ's attitude to suffering?

There is little we can do to stop darkness descending, but there is a lot we can do to discover its hidden treasures. So whenever you find yourself in a place of darkness, hold fast to the idea that what matters is not so much what is happening to you as the meaning that you can discover in it. Sorrows, griefs, losses, disappointments, frustrations, sickness, failures – these can be dark and difficult experiences. They can, however, be times of spiritual growth and development, providing we stand up to them with the right attitude. And the right attitude is this – God will allow nothing to come into my life unless it can be used.

If you say to yourself, 'This should not have happened to me because I am a child of God,' then your attitude will prevent you from discovering the treasures that are all around. When you realise that you can use everything, then you need not be afraid of anything.

**O Father, help me to have the right attitude to all my circumstances, for then I can learn rather than live in fear. When I serve You, then all things serve me. I am so grateful. Amen.**

# 'Grace enough, and to spare'

### FOR READING & MEDITATION - COLOSSIANS 4:7-18

'I, Paul, write this greeting in my own hand. Remember my chains.
Grace be with you.' (v.18)

**S**ome years ago, a friend of mine who was passing through a time of darkness said to me, 'Can you help me out of this darkness?' After talking with him for a few moments, I saw clearly that the darkness he was in was something that he would have to go through for a little while longer. So I said to him, 'I can't help you get out of the darkness, but I can help to get the darkness out of you.' His eyes lit up and he said, 'Quickly, tell me how.' I was not able to give him any 'quick' answers, but I was able to give him clear directions – directions that enabled him to find treasures in his darkness. Many of those directions I will share with you in the remaining days of the year.

**FURTHER STUDY**

Acts 16:23-34;
2 Cor. 12:7-10

1. How did Paul respond to suffering and imprisonment?

2. What happens when we are weak?

In the text before us today, Paul shows how he had developed the attitude that enabled him to stand fast in the midst of the most dark and depressing circumstances. Listen to the words again, this time in the Moffatt translation: 'This salutation is in my own hand, from Paul. "Remember I am in prison. Grace be with you."' We might have expected Paul to have written: 'I am in prison; God give me grace.' But no, he puts it the other way round: 'I am in prison; grace be with *you*.' It is as if he is saying, 'I have found grace in the darkness of a prison experience – enough and to spare. I pass it on to you.'

The experience of being engulfed in darkness can either make or break us. Some it shatters; others it strengthens. When our souls are open to the grace that constantly flows towards us from heaven, then every limitation, every difficult situation, every perplexing circumstance can be the setting for a new discovery of God and a new revelation of His love.

**O Father, help me whenever I am engulfed in darkness to find grace - and not only grace enough for my need but 'enough to spare'. May its flow contribute to my overflowing. I ask this in and through the peerless and precious name of Jesus. Amen.**

# Is darkness God's punishment?

**FOR READING & MEDITATION – JOHN 15:1-17**

'… every branch that does bear fruit he prunes so that it will be even more fruitful.' (v.2)

I pause in our meditations to make it clear that the darkness I am discussing here is not the cloud of guilt that descends upon us because of some sin we have committed, but the darkness allowed by God to deepen our understanding of Him and His love. We live in a world of moral consequences, and sin does produce darkness in the soul, but if, when we are in darkness, there is no conscious sin in our lives, we ought not to beat ourselves over the head with a spiritual club and say, 'This is happening to me because I am such an awful person.' You should see the darkness from the same perspective as the poet who said:

**FURTHER STUDY**

Mark 14:3;
John 12:1-3;
2 Cor. 2:14-17

1. What was the result of breaking the jar?
2. What does God do through us?

*Why do I creep along the heavenly way*
*By inches in the garish day?*
*Last night when darkest clouds did round me lower*
*I strode whole leagues in one short hour!*

*Mary G. Slocum (1851–?)*

The dark clouds of difficult circumstances can cause us to run into the arms of God. It is often at times when we feel deep pain and grief that we turn to the One who was there all along, waiting to be known and waiting to comfort and help us.

In the Garden of Gethsemane, Jesus brought His pain and anguish to His Father. He still had to face the cross, but because He did, the world was never the same again. As Samuel Chadwick said, 'It's wonderful what God can do with a broken heart, if He gets all the pieces.'

If at this moment you find yourself in darkness and your heart is broken and dispirited, then give God all the pieces. He is more than able to put your life together again, perhaps in a new and more glorious pattern.

**Father, help me to learn the important spiritual lesson that every branch in You that bears fruit is pruned that it might bear more fruit. Prune me that I might be more fruitful. In Jesus' name I ask it. Amen.**

# CWR Ministry Events

## PLEASE PRAY FOR THE TEAM

| DATE | EVENT | PLACE | PRESENTER(S) |
|---|---|---|---|
| 3 Nov | Christians @ Work | Waverley Abbey House | Beverley Shepherd |
| 9 Nov | Understanding Yourself, Understanding Others MBTI® Basic (for counselling students) | WAH | Lynn & Andrew Penson |
| 10 Nov | Deeper Insights into MBTI® | WAH | Lynn & Andrew Penson |
| 19-21 Nov | Revelation Bible Discovery Weekend | WAH | Philip Greenslade |
| 19-23 Nov | Introduction to Biblical Care and Counselling | Pilgrim Hall | Angie Coombes, Richard Laws & team |
| 24 Nov | Insight into Depression | PH | Chris Ledger |
| 30 Nov | How to Help Couples with Troubled Marriages | WAH | Heather & Ian Churchill |
| 4 Dec | Women's Christmas Celebration | PH | Lynn Penson & Abby Guinness |
| 5 Dec | The Life and Times of Jesus | WAH | Andy Peck |
| 23-27 Dec | Christmas House Party | PH | Steve & Sandra Piggott |

Please also pray for students and tutors on our ongoing **BA in Counselling** programme at Waverley and Pilgrim Hall and our **Certificate and Diploma of Christian Counselling** and **MA in Integrative Psychotherapy** held at London School of Theology.

For further details and a full list of CWR's courses, phone +44 (0)1252 784719, or visit the CWR website at **www.cwr.org.uk** Pilgrim Hall **www.pilgrimhall.com**

# Never alone

FOR READING & MEDITATION - 1 CORINTHIANS 10:1-13
'And God is faithful; he will not let you be tempted beyond
what you can bear.' (v.13)

**T**oday we ask ourselves: what are some of the dark and difficult experiences through which we are called to pass, and how do we go about discovering treasure in darkness? The first of life's situations which we focus on is the darkness of a persistent and oppressive temptation. Perhaps at this very moment you are engulfed by a cloud of temptation that threatens to destabilise your spiritual equilibrium. Take heart, today's text tells us that God is committed to standing with you in the hour of temptation and providing a way of escape for you. You will find treasure in the darkness.

**FURTHER STUDY**

Luke 4:1-15

1. How did Jesus overcome temptation?

2. What was the result?

Note again what the text says: 'God is faithful; he will not let you be tempted beyond what you can bear.' God owes it to Himself, His Word, His love and His character to help you in any temptation that comes your way. He knows that you can do nothing without Him and that you will certainly fail if He abandons you, so the Almighty will not let you down. Quite simply, the truth is this – if God were to remove Himself from you in the moments when you are overtaken by powerful and oppressive temptation, He would be untrue to Himself. So right now, let your soul find reassurance and encouragement in this revelation – He has promised to stand by you and there is no way He will ever abandon you because He cannot be untrue to Himself.

But what does this faithfulness mean? It does not mean that He will prevent the darkness of temptation from descending; what it does mean is that He will never allow the temptation to go beyond your power to resist. That's the escape route He promises. Rest in that promise – He will never fail.

**O Father, I am so thankful that when I enter into the darkness of temptation I am never alone. No matter how powerful the temptation, You will never allow it to get beyond my ability to resist. I am deeply grateful. Amen.**

# Unbeatable and unbreakable

THURS
8 NOV

**FOR READING & MEDITATION - ISAIAH 54:11-17**

'... no weapon forged against you will prevail ...' (v.17)

We continue examining the subject of finding treasures in the darkness of fierce and oppressive temptation. As we saw, one treasure is the discovery that God always keeps His promises. How could we ever understand the faithfulness of God unless we saw it at work in difficult and distressing situations?

Temptation, though you may not think so when you are going through it, can have a useful and beneficial purpose. Goethe said, 'Difficulties prove men.' As we grapple, we grow. The greatest treasure we can discover in the darkness of temptation is the understanding that we can do more with temptation than just bear it – we can use it. The secret of using temptation and turning it to our advantage is one of life's greatest treasures. Once we have learned it we are unbeatable and unbreakable. And it is one of those priceless treasures that can only be found in the dark.

A Sunday school teacher told me that when she was talking to her class about the cross a little boy raised his hand and said, 'Jesus didn't just carry His cross – He used it.' What a powerful truth lies in the words of that little boy. God does not want us just to bear a cross of temptation; He wants us to use it. A stoic bears a cross; a Christian uses it and makes it bear him.

I once heard the singer Sammy Davis Jr take words that were shouted to him from the audience and put them to music. Someone handed him a shopping list which he promptly set to a tune. Everything can be used – even temptation. So before going any further, settle for this as a life conviction – it's not what comes, it's what we do with it, that's important.

**FURTHER STUDY**

Psa. 119:130;
Isa. 60:1-7; 61:1-7

1. What is over people and what is over us?

2. What does God give us for ashes, mourning and despair?

**Father, I see so clearly that when I am in You and You are in me, then everything can be used - even temptation. Help me to discover even more of the treasures that lie in its oppressive darkness. In Jesus' name I pray. Amen.**

# 'It hurts good'

**FOR READING & MEDITATION – JAMES 1:1-8**

'Consider it pure joy, my brothers, whenever you face trials
of many kinds ...' (v.2)

**W**e are saying that when we find ourselves engulfed by the darkness of fierce and oppressive temptation, we ought not to allow ourselves to sink back in despondency and say, 'Why should this happen to me?' but remind ourselves that the darkness contains hidden treasures.

Philosophers have told us repeatedly that life is determined more by our reactions than by our actions. Temptation sweeps in upon us and forces its way into our lives without asking (and sometimes without our acting) and it is then that our reaction plays an important part. We can react in self-pity and frustration, or we can act with confidence and courage and let the temptation cause us to sink down even more deeply into the everlasting arms. If you have been seeing temptation as a groaning .point, change your perspective and begin to view it as a growing point.

**FURTHER STUDY**

2 Cor. 4:13-18;
Rev. 3:7-13,21

1. What do our troubles achieve?

2. What has God promised to those who overcome?

I am told that whenever they are sick, some Native South Americans push aside modern medicines that are available, preferring instead the medicines that their ancestors have used down the centuries. One reporter was told, 'The trouble with modern medicine is that it is not bitter and we are suspicious of anything that does not cause us distaste.' They have a saying which they use when taking their bitter medicines: 'It hurts good.' You can make temptation 'hurt good' when you see it as an opportunity to increase your dependence upon God, develop your trust, improve your character and make you more and more like Jesus. The darkness yields a treasure – a deeper awareness and understanding of the importance of absolute dependence on an all-sufficient God.

**Lord Jesus, You who faced the bitterness of a wilderness temptation and used it in the purposes of redemption, teach me to do the same. May I face the bitter in the assurance that when You are with me all it can do is make me better. Amen.**

**FOR READING & MEDITATION - JAMES 1:9-20**

'Blessed is the man who perseveres under trial ...' (v.12)

Today we face the question: why does God allow temptation? One way to gain understanding is to look at the Greek word for temptation – *peirasmos* – which means to test, to try or to prove. The biblical use of the word (unlike the modern use of it) does not contain the idea of entrapment but rather, putting a person to a test for the purpose of deepening his or her qualities of character.

The purpose, then, behind every temptation which God allows is the development of character. One writer says, 'The conversion of a soul is the work of a moment but the making of a saint is the work of a lifetime.' Oswald Chambers, expressing the same truth in a different way, said, 'God can, in one single moment, make a heart pure, but not even God can in a single moment give a person character.' Character would not be the precious thing it is if it could be acquired without struggle, without combat and without contradictions. Virtue that has not been tried and tested in the fire is not worthy of the name of virtue. In a world such as this, it is essential that temptation should come to try us, for without it there can be no advance in virtue, no growth in holiness and no development in character.

## FURTHER STUDY

Gen. 39:1-12; 2 Sam. 11:2-14

1. How was Joseph's character revealed?

2. Contrast the characters of David and Uriah.

But what is character? The definition I like, and which I have used before, is this: 'Character is what we are in the dark' (D.L. Moody). Reputation is what others think of us – character is what we are on the inside. It is the strength of soul we develop as we stand against the tide of temptation. As I said the other day, when we grapple, we grow. And out of the growing comes character.

**O Father, if character is something slowly achieved rather than suddenly acquired, help me in the achieving of it. And if temptation is a way of deepening my personal qualities, then I welcome it. Help me to turn it all to good. In Jesus' name. Amen.**

# A purpose in all things

**FOR READING & MEDITATION – 1 PETER 1:1-9**

'These have come so that your faith ... may be proved genuine ...'
(v.7)

To many people, Christians included, the idea that God allows His children to be tempted by the devil is an idea that is inconsistent with His might and omnipotence. 'If God is Almighty,' they reason, 'then He should intervene in Satan's attempts to seduce us and should prevent Satan damaging or destroying our personalities.' But it is because God is omnipotent that He permits us to be tempted.

P. Harton says, 'A conquering nation that is not sure of its own strength, refuses the people any kind of independence at all, and keeps control with a strong hand, is governed not by a love for the people but by a fear of the people.' God does not control the lives of His people by fear but by love, justice and the desire always to do what is right. He will not deliver us from temptation, but He can deliver us in it. Whenever we are faced with dilemma, it is one of Satan's strategies to persuade us that because God does not deliver us from temptation, He is not able to help us. I tell you, with all the force and conviction of my being – God is well able to help us, and the help He gives us is not to extricate us from the temptation but to supply us with the grace to face it.

**FURTHER STUDY**

Prov. 17:3;
Isa. 48:10;
Dan. 3:13-30

1. Why is affliction like a furnace?

2. How was the faith of the Hebrews tested and rewarded?

So if temptation can be used for our spiritual development, why fear it? Humility will not permit us to desire temptation – that would be to presume on our own strength – but eagerness for our Christian advancement should result in our not dreading it and not being surprised when it comes. Holiness and purity of soul would not be as awesome as they are to our human reasoning if they could be acquired without a struggle and without commitment.

**My Father and my God, thank You for unveiling to me the treasures that are hidden in the darkness of temptation. Help me in future to face all temptation in the sure knowledge that You can provide the grace to overcome it. In Jesus' name. Amen.**

# Join '**The Big Thank You**' for Past, Present and Future

**We're celebrating 25 years at Waverley Abbey House, and there's a lot to thank God for ...**

### PAST – MANY LIVES CHANGED

Over 35,000 students trained, hundreds of books translated into over 50 languages, over 85,000 books and DVDs sent into prisons, at least 200,000 new Christians resourced with Bible-based material. And so much more ...

### PRESENT – A SIGNIFICANT YEAR

We're thankful that Waverley Abbey House is full to capacity with students, that we have our first fully university accredited course (BA Hons in Counselling) and we've established a new campus, Pilgrim Hall. Exciting new ministry developments continue in South East Asia.

### FUTURE – REVIVAL STARTS HERE

Our vision: to establish a Christian university, training Christian professionals to bring the living water of the Spirit into the secular arena. We long for a tidal wave of God's presence to engulf this spiritually dry nation, through our courses and resources.

### A SPECIAL OFFERING

Please consider taking part in our 25 Year Thank Offering, to thank God for all He's done in the past and for all He is still doing. **Your gift – large or small – will also help ensure the ongoing work of CWR**.

Ever thankful

*Mick Brooks*

**Mick Brooks**
CWR's Chief Executive

**Please fill in the '25th Anniversary Thanks Offering' section on the order form at the back of this publication, completing the Gift Aid declaration if appropriate.**

# Our most vulnerable moment

**FOR READING & MEDITATION - MATTHEW 11:20-30**

'Come to me, all you who are weary and burdened,
and I will give you rest.' (v.28)

**W**e look today at another form of darkness which at one time or another almost everyone has to face – the darkness of bereavement. In the very nature of things, hundreds of you reading these lines will be there right now. Others may have to face bereavement in the very near future, so we must learn how to live in this darkness with the confidence that there are treasures to be found even here.

A fact that has always struck me whenever I have been with people who are in bereavement is that no matter how strong they may be at other times, whenever they are bereaved they become extremely vulnerable and thus open either to pain or consolation. I have spoken before of the American financier who was regarded as a tough and callous man. Yet when his wife died, he was so distraught that he cried out, 'Won't someone please give me some comfort?' How human that is!

**FURTHER STUDY**

Isa. 55:1-7;
John 7:37-39

1. What does God promise to those who come to Him?

2. How does Jesus link inflow and outflow of life?

Let's examine some of the 'comforts' which the world offers to those who are bereaved. One is to drown one's sorrows in drink. Many faced with the loss of a loved one try to find refuge by soaking themselves in alcohol. Wanting to soften the pain inside them, they take what seems to be the easiest way to that end. But this is not the way. In the first place, it may lead us to act in a way we might later regret, and in the second, it is thoroughly ineffective to offer long-term relief. There is always the morning after, and the poignant memories return to haunt the mind – again and again and again. There is no true comfort in the 'cup that cheers' – lasting comfort comes only through Christ.

**Father, help me to learn that there can be no escaping from reality, but with You I can face anything that comes, knowing that though You will not save me from it, You will save me in it. I am deeply grateful. Thank You, dear Father. Amen.**

# Supplements are not solutions

## FOR READING & MEDITATION - ISAIAH 26:1-11

'You will keep in perfect peace him whose mind is steadfast,
because he trusts in you.' (v.3)

We continue looking at the various kinds of comfort which the world offers to those who are bereaved, and today we look first at the comfort that comes from books. Some time ago I was shown a statement made by a well-known 'Agony Aunt' who has a regular column in a women's magazine. She was giving advice to someone who had been bereaved, and this is what she wrote: 'Find comfort in literature. The anodyne you need is good reading. Go along to your local library and get a good book. Lose yourself in it and you will find that it will do for you what it does for countless others – brings relief to your aching heart.'

I have no doubt that this advice is well-meaning, but the worth of it can only be judged by those who love books. And not everyone does. People who have little interest in literature would find little help in this advice. A book can be a wonderful extra to those who need comfort, but it is absurd to expect a piece of literature to heal a wounded spirit.

Another way of the world is to recommend that one turn to nature. Lord Avebury, in his preface to his two volumes, *The Marvels of the Universe*, says, 'Nature does much to soothe and comfort and console.' I do not deny that there is a healing touch in nature. Multitudes who have been bereaved have gone out into the hills and felt ministered to by the power of nature, but once again, though it is a good supplement, nature is not a good substitute for the precious and powerful comfort that flows from Christ.

Art, nature, literature – all these may have a part to play in the life of those who are bereaved. They can help, but Jesus alone can heal.

## FURTHER STUDY

Isa. 61:1-6;
Jer. 6:13-15

1. What was to be the ministry of the Messiah?

2. Why did God reprimand the prophets and priests?

**Lord Jesus Christ, I am grateful for the supplements that can help me in the hour of need, but help me see that they are only supplements and they can never be a substitute for You. I glance at them, but my gaze must be ever upon You. Amen.**

# 'Vita! Vita! Vita!'

### FOR READING & MEDITATION - JOHN 6:35-51

'... everyone who looks to the Son and believes in him shall have eternal life, and I will raise him up ...' (v.40)

The central thought I want to share with you today is one that I wish I could write on the sky in letters of fire so that the whole world might see. It is this – *the Christian faith is the only faith that lights up that dark area of life which we call death.* And it lights it up, not with a word, but with the Word made flesh. Jesus went through death, and thus the word of resurrection became flesh in Him. As it was said of Emerson, 'He did not argue; he just let in the light,' so it can be said of Jesus, He did not argue immortality; He simply showed Himself alive.

**FURTHER STUDY**

1 Cor. 15:20-23, 50-58;
1 Thess. 4:13-18

1. How can we be encouraged in the face of death?

2. Why can we be certain of life after death?

I have told the story before of a missionary who was teaching a group of children about the cross and death of Jesus. As the time had gone, she was forced to end the story at the point where Jesus was laid in the grave. A little boy jumped into the aisle and said, 'It's not fair – he was a good man.' One little girl, who knew the full story, pulled him back to his seat and said, 'Ssh! Don't make a fuss – He didn't stay dead.' Well, if he didn't *stay* dead, neither will we stay dead.

A biographer says of Tennyson, 'He laid his mind on the mind of others and they believed his beliefs.' This is what our Lord does, only in an infinitely greater way – He lays His mind upon ours and we believe in His beliefs. And our Lord believed in and demonstrated immortality. No wonder the early Christians, locked up within the dark underground prisons, wrote on the walls, 'Vita! Vita! Vita!' – 'Life! Life! Life!' Prison walls could not quench or stifle this life, nor can death extinguish it. Can death stop a Christian? Stop him? It only frees him – for ever.

O Jesus, Saviour and Lord, You have laid Your mind upon my mind so that now I believe Your beliefs. You believed in eternal life and demonstrated it - so now, do I. I shall write on all my confining walls - 'Vita! Vita! Vita!' Amen.

# When diamonds look their best

**FOR READING & MEDITATION - DEUTERONOMY 33:24-29**

'The eternal God is your refuge, and underneath are the everlasting arms.' (v.27)

Now that we have looked at some of the ineffective comforts that the world offers to those who are bereaved, and the sure confidence Scripture gives us that, in Jesus, death has been defeated, we are ready to ask ourselves: what are some of the treasures we might find in the darkness of bereavement?

It is now several years since I laid my wife to rest, and I have been asking myself what treasures I discovered in the darkness of my own bereavement. One that immediately comes to mind is a new discovery of God and the truths contained in His Word. I had walked with the Lord for 40 years before my wife was taken from me by cancer, and I had thought my intimacy with God was about as good as it could ever be. I found, however, that the death of my wife produced in me a degree of grief and sorrow that I had never thought possible. I had known for several months that my wife's condition meant that her death was imminent, but I was not prepared for the shock wave that went over me when it actually took place.

The text I have chosen for today is one that had always been a great favourite of mine, but now, since I have passed through the darkness of bereavement, it has taken on a dimension that is almost impossible for me to describe. Just as a precious diamond is best seen against a dark velvet background, so does the truth of God shine more beautifully when set against those black moments of life such as death and bereavement. The truth of God shines most beautifully at any time, but believe me, never more illustriously than when set against the darkness of a bitter and heart-rending experience.

## FURTHER STUDY

Psa. 23:1-6; Isa. 63:7-9

1. Why did the psalmist not fear in the shadow of death?

2. What happens when God's people are distressed?

**Father, I see that grief and sadness can be the backdrop and setting against which Your truth and comfort shine more beautifully than ever. Help me, whenever I am engulfed by such feelings, to expect and await a new discovery of You. Amen.**

# Grace that abounds

'And God is able to make all grace abound to you ... so that ...
you will abound in every good work.' (v.8)

**W**e saw yesterday that one of the treasures we are likely to find in the darkness of bereavement is a new discovery of God and a new understanding of His Word. We may think we understand a truth of Scripture, but we will never really understand it until that truth is the only thing we have left to hold on to. Deuteronomy 33:27 (the text we looked at yesterday) was always a favourite of mine, but now it is more than a favourite text – it is a spiritual lifeline. I know its truth in a way I never knew it before, because it held me in one of the darkest moments of my experience – bereavement.

**FURTHER STUDY**

Matt. 5:1-12;
Rom. 12:9-16

1. What is God's promise to those who mourn?

2. What is our responsibility to those who mourn?

Another treasure that we can find in this type of darkness is a more effective spiritual contribution to the life of the Church. Out of our personal sorrow comes a sensitivity and a concern for others that impacts their lives in a greater way than ever before. A couple of years after my wife died, a woman said to me, 'I used to listen to you 20 years ago when you were a pastor in London, and although I was blessed by what you said, I always felt you were too demanding of us and a little hard. Now you are so different. The hardness has gone and a wonderful softness flows out of you.' I tell you, a tear came to my eye as she talked, because I recognised the truth of what she was saying. People tell me that following my bereavement there has been a new note in my writings, in my preaching, and in my teaching. This is the treasure I found in my darkness.

If you are bereaved at this moment, or facing a possible bereavement, take heart – you will find treasures in the darkness that will remain with you for the rest of your life. He gives most when most is taken away.

**Father, the need for consolation lies deep within me and is therefore inescapable. But help me understand also that while You meet me in grief, You want to take me beyond it - to a greater understanding of and usefulness for You. Amen.**

# 'Mankind's biggest problem'

## FOR READING & MEDITATION – PSALM 91:1-16

'I will say of the LORD, "He is my refuge and my fortress, my God, in whom I trust."' (v.2)

Yet another form of darkness in which people sometimes find themselves is the darkness of loneliness. Can divine treasures be discovered there? With all my heart I say – they can.

By 'loneliness' I don't mean 'aloneness'. It must be understood at once that there is a great difference between loneliness and aloneness: it is possible to be alone and yet not lonely. The psychiatrist and author Dr Leonard Zunin said, 'Loneliness is mankind's biggest problem and is the major reason behind the many and varied symptoms which I see in the people who present themselves before me day after day.' So what is loneliness? It is the feeling we get when we are bereft of meaningful human companionship; it is a sense of isolation, of inner emptiness, deprivation and worthlessness.

**FURTHER STUDY**

Psa. 88:1-18

1. Identify the psalmist's emotions.

2. What did he say about friends?

The poet Rupert Brooke records how, when he first set sail from Liverpool for New York, on 22 May 1913, he felt terribly lonely because no one had come to see him off. Everyone else had friends waving them goodbye – but not he. Looking down from the deck, he saw a scruffy little boy and swift as thought he ran down the gangway and said to him, 'Will you wave to me if I give you sixpence?' 'Why, yes,' said the little boy. The sixpence changed hands and that day Rupert Brooke wrote in his diary, 'I got my sixpenceworth in an enthusiastic farewell – dear, dear boy.'

Those who have never felt the pangs of loneliness will find it hard to understand a story like that. But to others it will carry a world of meaning. It is a desolating experience to be lonely, yet the divine Presence can so reveal itself that even this deep darkness is made bearable.

**O Father, help me understand that whenever I feel alone, forsaken or forgotten – in truth I am not alone, for You are constantly with me. May I know the reality of this day by day. In Jesus' name I ask it. Amen.**

# Take Your Church on a Jo

Many churches in 2012 have embarked on a 'Journey of Discovery' to read the entire Bible in a year using *Cover to Cover Complete*, CWR's one-year chronological reading plan incorporating the full Bible text. One participant remarks:

> '*Cover to Cover Complete* has undoubtedly helped increase self-discipline in the reading of Scripture, enabled people to get to know the Bible better and, indeed, some now want to go study it in greater depth'
> Peter Hinton, St James' Church, Alderholt

**NEW FOR 2012**

This year, CWR has republished *Cover to Cover Complete* using, for the first time, the New International Version 2011. The text is divided into manageable daily sections, and charts, maps, illustrations, diagrams and timelines enhance understanding of the Bible and biblical times. Each day ends with a devotional thought written by Selwyn Hughes and Trevor Partridge.

If your church would like to consider going on a 'Journey of Discovery', why not start in 2013?

BRAND-NEW
EDITION
INCORPORATING
FULL
NIV TEXT

# ...ney of Discovery in 2013!

We have a number of resources available to help promote the *Cover to Cover Complete* Bible-reading programme in your church. When you register, you will receive:

- promotional posters
- invitation cards to distribute
- details of special discounts for churches.

Place your order during November and December for a 1 January start. Along with your copies of *Cover to Cover Complete*, you'll receive bookmarks for each individual and all you need to access your church's very own online discussion forum.

**Is your church ready for a 'Journey of Discovery'?**
**For more information/to register your church and receive a FREE welcome pack, visit www.cwr.org.uk/journey or call 01252 784782 or crm@cwr.org.uk**

# No one as lonely as He

**FOR READING & MEDITATION - MATTHEW 26:36-56**

'Then all the disciples deserted him and fled.' (v.56)

**W**e said yesterday that there is a great difference between loneliness and aloneness. It is possible to be alone and yet not feel lonely. To feel lonely can be quite terrifying. The feeling of loneliness is not diminished in a crowd, or, for that matter, in a church. Someone has described some churches – thankfully not all – as 'lonely places where lonely people go so that everyone can be lonely together'. One can be *in* a crowd and not *of* it.

Did Jesus ever feel lonely? I cannot think that He would be able to sympathise with this problem had He not at some time in His life felt lonely. There were times when He was bereft of human companionship, and in that dark hour on the cross He was bereft of divine companionship, too. The disciples, it seems, were incapable of entering into Jesus' feelings as He agonised in the Garden of Gethsemane – how would He have felt about that, I wonder? On the eve of His death they argued about precedence; they slept while He wrestled in prayer; when He was arrested, they ran away. Most who have been willing to die for a cause have been able to comfort themselves that there were those who sympathised with them – but even this was denied Jesus. His self-sacrifice mystified the people who were His closest companions. Not one single soul understood why He allowed men to take Him and string Him up on a cross.

**FURTHER STUDY**

Psa. 22:1-8; 41:1-9; Matt. 27:45-46

1. What did the psalmist prophesy of Jesus?

2. Why did the psalmist feel especially rejected?

However difficult it may be to face the darkness of loneliness, we know one thing at least – Jesus knows how it feels. Others may not be able to understand it, but He most certainly does.

**Lord Jesus, clearly no one has ever touched some depths of loneliness in the way You have. Draw close to me in my own moments of loneliness, so that I might learn how to find the treasures in its darkness. For Your own dear name's sake. Amen.**

# More of God

### FOR READING & MEDITATION - MATTHEW 28:16-20

'And surely I am with you always, to the very end of the age.' (v.20)

If, as we have been saying, there are treasures to be found in darkness, what is the treasure that can be discovered in the depths of loneliness? It may sound trite to some, but the answer is this – a deeper sense of the presence of God. An acquaintance of mine, a preacher who never married and who spends a great deal of time on his own, said this: 'Loneliness, that precious opportunity for discovering more of God.' He went on to say that he noticed that the times of his deepest loneliness were the times when Christ was most real to him.

F.W. Robertson, a preacher of the nineteenth century, proved this. He was bitterly attacked by other Christians for his views, and as his brief life sped away his friends got fewer and fewer. It was in one of these dark periods, when it seemed that all his friends had gone, that he wrote, 'I am alone, lonelier than ever, sympathised with by none, because I sympathise too much with all, but the All sympathises with me ... I turn from everything to Christ. I get glimpses into His mind, and I am sure that I love Him more and more. A sublime feeling of His presence comes about me at times which makes inward solitariness a trifle to talk about.'

**FURTHER STUDY**

Heb. 13:5-6;
Acts 23:9-11

1. What can we say with confidence?

2. What was Paul's experience in confinement?

Look at that last sentence again: 'A sublime feeling of His presence comes about me ... which makes inward solitariness a trifle to talk about.' What a testimony! He found treasure in the darkness. With the assurance of Christ's presence vouchsafed to every Christian, there need not be utter loneliness in the hearts of God's children. Jesus walked that way so that no one need ever walk it again.

**Father, I see that though I might feel lonely, I need not feel desolate, for You are ever with me. Show me how to drop all my barriers so that You can enter into the deepest depths of my being. In Jesus' name I ask it. Amen.**

# Pause – and consider

**FOR READING & MEDITATION – ROMANS 12:1-21**

'Share with God's people who are in need. Practise hospitality.' (v.13)

It would be impossible to discuss the subject of loneliness properly without considering that some people bring loneliness upon themselves – they are lonely through their own actions and attitudes. 'Loneliness', says one writer, 'is more of an attitude than a circumstance; more self-inflicted than outwardly caused. It is not just a matter of isolation, it is more a matter of insulation. Lonely people build walls around themselves and then complain of their loneliness.' We can sometimes be so concerned with ourselves and the way *we* feel things should be, that others find it difficult to be around us.

**FURTHER STUDY**

Job 2:11-13;
Prov. 18:24;
Eccl. 4:7-12

1. How can we be a good friend?

2. Why are friendships vital?

Those who, like myself, find themselves in circumstances that compel them to live alone, must watch that they do not become morose, critical, self-pitying and inward-looking. These attitudes will reinforce even the slightest feelings of loneliness and quickly drive people away. 'In a needy world like ours,' said one preacher, 'anybody can have friendship who will give it.' And Emerson said many years ago, 'The only way to have a friend is to be a friend.' When anyone says, 'I am friendless,' he or she comes dangerously near to self-condemnation. The statement begs the rejoinder, 'Have you *been* a friend?'

The Greek word *charis*, usually translated in the New Testament as 'grace', also means 'charm'. God's grace can add charm to any disposition. Have you noticed how two people in love sometimes become radiant? They not only demonstrate love to each other, but it spills over to everyone else as well. Christ's presence in your heart will help you to be a friend, and being a friend means you will never have to concern yourself about having a friend.

**Father, help me to be open to the fact that sometimes my feelings of loneliness might be self-induced. If this is so, give me the courage to change. Illumine my life with Your friendship, and then help me to pass it on to others. Amen.**

# Where do you live?

**FOR READING & MEDITATION - ACTS 17:22-34**

'For in him we live and move and have our being.' (v.28)

**W**e continue to explore the idea that there are treasures to be found in even the deepest darkness – loneliness being no exception. We must be careful, however, that in looking for the treasures that lie in the darkness of loneliness we don't make the mistake of pretending that loneliness is not a painful experience. There are some Christians who, whenever they sense there is pain in an experience, pull away from it and pretend that it is not painful at all. That is an escape into unreality. Loneliness can be pretty painful and if it is, don't pretend that it is not. Christianity is not a religion of pretence; it is a religion of reality. We face the pain knowing that Jesus can help us through it and turn the pain into something of benefit to Him, to others and to ourselves. The important thing is to recognise that in all pain there is potential. And the art is to admit the pain but focus on the potential.

And what is the potential of loneliness? What are the hidden treasures that lie within its darkness? The hurt or the pain brings deeper sensitivity to the problems of others, greater awareness of God's tenderness and nearness, increased self-understanding and the realisation that out of every pain God can produce a pearl. A visitor to a nursing home saw a man he knew, a Christian, and said to him, 'I'm sorry to see you living in this nursing home.' The old man drew himself up to his full height and said, 'My friend, I do not live in a nursing home – I live in God.'

What about you, my lonely friend? Where do you live? All alone – or in God?

**FURTHER STUDY**

Psa. 71:1-8;
Phil. 3:20;
Heb. 11:13-16

1. How did the psalmist refer to the Lord?

2. Where do we belong?

**O Father, sweep into my soul with such a consciousness of Your presence that although I may be bereft of human companionship, loneliness will be a minor problem and not a major one. This I ask in and through my Saviour's precious name. Amen.**

# 'Music in the making'

**FOR READING & MEDITATION - HABAKKUK 2:1-4**

'For the revelation awaits an appointed time ...
Though it linger, wait for it ...' (v.3)

**A**nother form of darkness in which some Christians on occasion find themselves is the darkness of spiritual silence. I mean by this those times when we enter a situation where it seems the heavens are silent and God no longer directs us. We are not conscious of any sin, we pray and read the Scriptures daily, but nothing we do seems to bring guidance for the next step forward. Is this where you are at the moment? Take heart – there are treasures to be found in even this darkness.

For some people, a period of spiritual silence is harder to bear than persecution or suffering. People who have been caught up in this have said to me, 'I can handle anything as long as I hear God's voice speaking to me, but when there is silence I find it hard, if not impossible, to cope.' But we must understand that a silent heaven does not mean an unconcerned heaven. There are always reasons for everything God does, and learning to trust these reasons even when we cannot understand them is one of the marks of spiritual maturity.

**FURTHER STUDY**

Lam. 3:17-28;
Dan. 9:1-14,23

1. Why could the prophet have hope?

2. How long was heaven silent when Daniel prayed?

Someone has said that pauses in music are 'music in the making'. A momentary pause in a musical composition produces a suspense that makes the music more beautiful than before. The pause prepares those who listen for finer music. I have sat with many who have thought that the period of spiritual silence in which they have found themselves was a sign of God's displeasure, but they came to see that the silence was really 'music in the making'. The music when it came was all the richer for the silence that preceded it.

**O Father, whenever I enter into the darkness of spiritual silence, teach me never to let go of what I learned in the light. Help me now to grasp the lesson that the silences are but 'music in the making'. In Jesus' name I pray. Amen.**

# 'The silent years'

**FOR READING & MEDITATION - GALATIANS 1:13-24**
'... I did not consult any man ... I went immediately into Arabia ...'
(vv.16-17)

**W**e often talk about the public life and ministry of Jesus, but little is said concerning what theologians call 'the silent years'. How the call to share the message that He was the Son of God must have burned in the Saviour's heart during His teens and twenties! Just picture it – the Son of God making yokes for the farmers of Israel, when He yearned to lift the yoke of sin from the neck of humanity; making ploughs to till the soil when He longed to plough deep furrows in the hearts of men and women. But this does not mean that He chafed or became impatient: clearly He knew that the silent years were a preparation for the great ministry that lay ahead of him. Thirty years of silence; three years of song. But, as I said yesterday, the song was all the richer for the silence that preceded it.

When I was in Nairobi some years ago, I met a man who described himself as a 'missionary casualty'. A 'missionary casualty' is someone who has to return from the mission field because of an inability to adjust. I asked him what had happened and he said, 'I decided to take a shortcut to learning the language by closing my text books and just going out among the people. I learned the language in a kind of way, but when I got into the midst of the people it was clear that I didn't make sense. They knew that I could not communicate in the way the other missionaries did and I did not have their ear. Gradually things got to me and I had a breakdown.'

He had longed to get among the people, but was not willing to bear the silence – hence he became unfruitful and unproductive. He was not prepared for the pause, and lived to regret it.

### FURTHER STUDY

Matt. 27:24-27;
1 Cor. 3:10-15

1. What happens when we take shortcuts?

2. What was Paul concerned to build?

**Father, I see that without a pause there is no 'music in the making'. Help me to understand that Your delays are not Your denials. The silences are working for me; treasures are to be found in the darkness. I believe it. Thank You, Father. Amen.**

# 'The prelude to the light'

**FOR READING & MEDITATION - HEBREWS 13:5-21**
'...Never will I leave you, never will I forsake you.' (v.5)

The thought that has been engaging our attention is that silence is 'music in the making'. Pauses create a suspense which makes the music even more lovely. I must be careful not to overwork the phrase 'music in the making' but permit me one last reference to it.

After many years of *Every Day with Jesus*, I think you will forgive me if I tell you of one of the many incidents that have come out of what I have written in its pages. A minister who was on the point of giving up the ministry because he was going through a period of spiritual silence,

**FURTHER STUDY**

Acts 1:1-14; 2:1-4

1. What were the disciples to do when Jesus ascended?

2. What was the result?

picked up a copy of *Every Day with Jesus* and read some words that I have used several times over the years (and referred to again at the beginning of this month): 'A dark tunnel is often the best way of getting round a hill.' He wrote, 'God used those words to show me that the darkness in which I was enveloped was really the prelude to the light. I had wanted to move on into something that I felt sure was the divine will, but every time I talked to God about it there was from His side nothing but silence. The words you wrote were like a new injection of life to my spirit and I held on, believing that when the light came I would find that God had been working for me in the darkness. One day the light shone and with such radiance that I could never have believed it possible. In that moment there was enough light to compensate for every hour of the darkness.'

And just as darkness is the prelude to the light, so is silence 'music in the making'. Never forget that God has music to play in your life which may not reach its full beauty if it is not preceded by a few silent pauses.

**Father, let this truth take hold of my inner being so that when I am next engulfed in darkness I may walk on in faith, knowing that the fact that I cannot hear You does not mean that I am forgotten by You. In Jesus' name I ask it. Amen.**

# The divine perspective

SUN
25 NOV

FOR READING & MEDITATION - JOB 23:1-17
'But he knows the way that I take; when he has tested me,
I shall come forth as gold.' (v.10)

We must not assume that because we are plunged into a period of silence we are being punished for something and God is no longer interested in us. It can mean, in fact, that we are right in the centre of the divine will.

Job was engulfed in silence and said, as we see in our passage for today, 'But if I go to the east, he is not there; if I go to the west, I do not find him. When he is at work in the north, I do not see him; when he turns to the south, I catch no glimpse of him' (vv.8–9). Here is a man suffering great physical affliction, bereft of his children, and harassed by a doubting wife. He is heavy of heart and goes out at night looking for God. He glances up into the heavens and says, 'I look and he is not there.' I think it is safe to say that perhaps no other human being (with the exception of our Lord Jesus Christ) experienced such deep darkness and desolating silence. When you have been through a time of silence such as Job went through, you know exactly what he is saying. However, in the midst of his darkness, Job says, 'But he knows the way that I take; when he has tested me, I shall come forth as gold.' How marvellous! Despite the silence, he has the right perspective.

**FURTHER STUDY**

2 Cor. 1:3–11;
4:7–12

1. What was Paul's human experience?

2. What was his divine perspective?

Listen again to what Job says: '*He* knows the way that I take.' *He!* I may not know, but He does – and that makes all the difference. If you are surrounded by darkness at this moment, then let the word that Job spoke those many centuries ago bring comfort and joy to your spirit. You may not know why you are going through this but *He* does. I promise you, if you can learn to look at life from God's point of view, then you have discovered the secret of everything.

**O Father, if your servant Job could do it, I can do it, too. From now on I will look at what is happening to my life, not from my point of view, but from Yours. Help me, not just today but every day. In Jesus' name I ask it. Amen.**

# The language of silence

**FOR READING & MEDITATION - ECCLESIASTES 3:1-14**
'... a time to be silent and a time to speak ...' (v.7)

**W**e spend one more day meditating on the thought that a time of spiritual silence does not necessarily mean that God is not interested in us. Susan Lenzkes, the author of the poems we use on the inside covers of *Every Day with Jesus*, talks in one of her books about 'the language of silence'. The point she makes is this – not all communication needs words. God has gifted us with words to convey our thoughts, but we communicate our feelings in many different ways – touch, tears, laughter, expression of the eyes, and so on. 'Sometimes words can be an intrusion,' she says, '– an obstacle.'

**FURTHER STUDY**

John 11:32-36; 13:1-5,14-15

1. Why did the Jews say that Jesus loved Lazarus?

2. How did Jesus communicate the principle of servanthood?

I am sure you have read the beautiful poem 'Footprints in the Sand' by Mary Stevenson. Mary's life was marked by hardship. She felt at times that God had left her and that she was engulfed in spiritual silence. One night she had a dream, which inspired her well-known poem. She was with God, looking back upon her life, which was portrayed as footprints along a sandy beach. Usually there were two sets of footprints – hers and the Saviour's. But as she looked more closely, along the very rugged places she saw only one set of footprints. Confused, she asked God if He had left her at those moments – moments when she needed Him the most. God replied with a no. When Mary saw the single set of footprints, they were His. Those were the times when He had picked her up and carried her.

Such is the language of love, wordless but sustaining, nevertheless. In the silence you may feel forgotten, but remember and realise that His arms are about you all the time. In periods of spiritual silence, God does not speak in words; He picks us up and holds us close.

**Thank you, Father, I needed to be reminded of this. Help me never to forget it and let me take comfort from the thought that You do not always communicate with words. You can reach me even in the silence. I am so deeply, deeply grateful. Amen.**

# A believer - and an achiever!

### FOR READING & MEDITATION - JOHN 20:19-31

'Thomas said to him, "My Lord and my God!"' (v.28)

**W**e turn now to consider another form of darkness which sometimes wraps itself around us – the darkness of deep and desolating doubts. Almost every Christian struggles at times with the problem of doubt. Some go through such agony of soul that they end up spiritually exhausted. I met someone not so long ago who told me, 'Things are happening at such a speed in the world, I'm afraid I'll wake up one day and find that science has completely disproved the Scriptures.' I assured her that her doubts were groundless, for scientific discovery should not be seen as being opposed to Scripture. Science can help to confirm what we read in Scripture. After all, the God of the Bible is the God who created the universe.

I suppose the classic example of doubt is the disciple Thomas. We call him 'doubting Thomas' – an unfair label if there ever was one. It's sad how we pick up what we consider a negative in a person and make him or her carry that label for a lifetime, or, in Thomas's case – two millennia. Thomas entered for a little while into the darkness of spiritual doubt, but he came out of that experience with a firmer faith than ever before. The darkness served only to deepen his love for Jesus. When I once visited Chennai, India, I heard of some of the treasures that came out of Thomas's darkness, as I was told how Thomas visited that continent and gave his life for the founding of a church which is there to this day. The 'St Thomas Christians', as they are called, are some of the finest believers I have ever met.

Thomas had his doubts allayed in one glorious moment of illumination. He became a believer and an achiever – and then he went places. So, my friend, can you!

## FURTHER STUDY

John 10:39-11:16; 14:5,
Acts 2:42-43; 5:12

1. Why do we think Thomas was overcome with negativity?

2. What did he achieve when his beliefs overcame his doubts?

**Gracious and loving Father, help me to understand that with You I can find treasures even in this darkness - the darkness of doubt. Show me how to turn this stumbling block into a stepping stone. In Jesus' name I ask it. Amen.**

# Truth – in the inner parts

**FOR READING & MEDITATION – PSALM 51:1-19**

'Surely you desire truth in the inner parts ...' (v.6)

**W**e continue looking at the problem of dark and desolating doubt. The first thing we should learn about doubt is the difference between defensive doubts and honest doubts. Some of the doubts that arise within us concerning our faith are unconscious attempts to hide some faults or failure.

Now not all doubts fall into this category, but many do. I have often talked to people, particularly young adults, who are committed to Jesus but are plagued with all kinds of doubts about the faith. On questioning them, I have found

**FURTHER STUDY**

Matt. 15:1-19;
Luke 18:18-25

1. Why were the Pharisees offended by Jesus?

2. Why did the ruler doubt Jesus' advice?

so many times that the doubts are really defensive attempts of the personality designed to relieve them of the responsibilities of their commitment.

Let me illustrate: I remember when I was a young Christian hearing a challenging sermon that showed me there was something about my Christian life that needed immediate correction. Then I came up against Brunner's Law: 'The more a decision will affect your way of life, the more your sinful nature will enter into the debate.' So what happened? My defensive carnal nature supplied me with doubts about the validity of

what I had heard, and I used these doubts to 'get me off the hook'. Rather than face the issue with which I was being challenged, I preferred the safety of doubt. It was only when my pastor said to me, 'If you believed the truth of what you heard, would there be anything in your life that would have to be changed?' that I saw what I was doing. I was using doubt as a defence. I preferred to believe that what I heard was not true because to believe it meant I had to change.

**O Father, whenever I am assailed by doubts, give me the ability to identify whether the doubt is a ploy of my personality or an honest and genuine concern. You desire 'truth in the inner parts'. So help me be honest. In Jesus' name I pray. Amen.**

# Our legacy from Adam

## FOR READING & MEDITATION - GENESIS 3:1-15
'But the Lord God called to the man, "Where are you?"' (v.9)

I want to spend another day on this issue of defensive doubts – doubts which our carnal nature provides us with so that we do not have to deepen our commitment. People of all ages are assailed by these kinds of doubts. Fallen human nature shrinks from facing up to God's challenges and it quickly fights back when we are caught in the challenge of moving on with God or staying where we are.

Deeply embedded in our nature is a defensive system that is a legacy from our first parents – Adam and Eve. Remember what happened immediately Adam and Eve sinned. God came down and confronted them with their sin. And what did they do? Instead of facing up to the issue as responsible human beings, they employed defensive manoeuvres in order to escape from the Creator's challenge. Adam said, 'The woman you put here with me – she gave me some fruit from the tree, and I ate it' (Gen. 3:12). Notice something that is often overlooked by Bible expositors here? Adam not only blamed his wife but also inferred that the predicament he found himself in was partly God's fault: 'The woman you put here with me – she gave me some fruit ...' Notice also how Eve handled the situation: 'The serpent deceived me ...' (3:13).

When caught defying God's principles, we are perfectly capable of using anything to protect ourselves – including doubt. How we need constantly to come before God, as shown in the words of Charles Wesley:

> Jesus the hindrance show
> Which I have feared to see,
> Yet let me now consent to know
> What keeps me out of Thee.

**FURTHER STUDY**

Gen. 4:8-12;
Num. 13:27-14:4

1. How was Cain like his father Adam?

2. Why did the people express doubt?

**Father, I see that my fallen human nature can be ruthlessly self-protective. Help me, therefore, to be ruthlessly honest. I ask it in and through our Lord's peerless and precious name. Amen.**

# Doubt – faith in two minds

**FOR READING & MEDITATION – ACTS 17:1-15**

'... they received the message with great eagerness and examined the Scriptures every day ...' (v.11)

**T**oday we examine the nature of honest doubts. Honest doubts are those doubts which arise from the difficult and perplexing situations in which we find ourselves and which appear to give the lie to the promises of God. For example, it is difficult sometimes to equate the truth of God's love with such things as natural disasters, physical suffering, child abuse and so on.

Some Christians attempt to resolve the problem of doubt by saying: 'A true believer ought not to doubt – that's the end of the matter.' What kind of answer is that? The truth is that sometimes we do doubt and we must face that fact, unpleasant though it may be. A painful crisis arises which doesn't seem to have any quick resolution and we wonder about all those promises of a prayer-answering God. Some particular part of Scripture (as we perceive it) does not stand up to our experience. The fellowship of the church lets us down and for a moment a doubt comes into our minds: 'Perhaps God will let me down, too.' These I regard as honest doubts; they arise in the hearts of even the most mature Christians.

**FURTHER STUDY**

Psa. 13:1-6; 43:1-5

1. How did the psalmist express both doubt and faith?

2. What questions did the psalmist ask?

Whenever you are assailed by honest doubts, remind yourself that doubt is not the same as unbelief. Os Guinness puts it like this: 'Doubt is a state of mind in suspension *between* faith and unbelief so that it is neither of them wholly and it is only each partly.' When we have an honest doubt, we are not betraying our faith or surrendering to unbelief. We are simply saying we are in two minds – and asking which way to go.

You can't stop doubts arising, but you can use it to ask questions which will enable you to take a firmer grip on God.

**Gracious and loving Father, what a relief it is to know that doubt is not the same as unbelief, but that it is faith in two minds. Help me in every period of doubt to make up my mind in conjunction with Your mind. In Jesus' name I ask it. Amen.**

# Bring your doubts to Jesus

## FOR READING & MEDITATION - MATTHEW 11:1-11

'Are you the one who was to come, or should we expect someone else?' (v.3)

**W**e ended yesterday with the thought that although we can't stop doubt arising in our minds, we can use it to ask questions that in turn will enable us to take a firmer grip on God. This is a treasure we can rescue from the darkness. Doubts can be valuable if they encourage us to search more deeply into God's Word for the answers which are surely there.

Unfortunately, in many of today's churches there is very little sympathy with those who doubt and raise what might seem like difficult questions. This is why Francis and Edith Schaeffer set up their ministry many years ago in a remote Swiss village. They established a centre for those with doubts about their faith and called it L'Abri, which is French for 'The Shelter'. Hundreds made their way there and came back with a faith deeper than ever before. Jesus did not reject Thomas because of his doubting attitude but said, 'Put your finger here; see my hands. Reach out your hand and put it into my side. Stop doubting and believe' (John 20:27). Has it ever struck you that John the Baptist, who witnessed the descent of the Holy Spirit upon Jesus and said, 'Look, the Lamb of God, who takes away the sin of the world!' (John 1:29), later entertained some doubts about Jesus? How did Jesus respond to those doubts? With love and sensitivity: 'Go back and report to John what you hear and see: The blind receive sight, the lame walk ...' (Matt. 11:4–5).

Those who doubt and use their doubts to ask deep questions of God and Scripture, will find themselves coming out with a faith stronger than ever before. Those who have doubted most, have become some of Jesus' most steadfast disciples. Treasures have been found in the darkness.

### FURTHER STUDY

Matt. 28:16-20;
Mark 9:15-27

1. How did Jesus respond to the disciples' doubts?

2. What did the boy's father do with his doubts?

**O Father, what a prospect - I can use all things to serve me, even doubt. Hold me fast whenever I am assailed by doubt so that I am able to doubt my doubts and believe my beliefs. In Christ's peerless and precious name. Amen.**

# Introduction to Biblical Care and Counselling

## A KEY COURSE IN CWR'S TRAINING PROGRAMME

Do you long to deal more successfully with life's issues and help other people to do the same? If so, may we encourage you to join us for our Introduction to Biblical Care and Counselling. Come and learn with our experienced teaching team the skills required to serve others effectively.

Given this opportunity to develop understanding and skills in pastoral care and counselling, but also to reflect on their own lives in the light of CWR's biblical model, many have found this five-day course life-transforming:

*'You arrive on the Monday as one person and gradually during the training you are completely transformed leaving on the Friday almost as if you have been reborn. I think the cost of the course is a life-time investment ...'*

*'Life-changing experience. Opens your eyes to God's character and his perfect plans and purposes.'*

*'It has been one of the most significant weeks of my life and really impacted my walk with God ... I would recommend it for anyone serving in the Church and hoping to become an instrument of God.'*

**WAVERLEY ABBEY HOUSE**

**PILGRIM HALL**

While the Introduction to Biblical Care and Counselling is a great course for anyone seeking personal and spiritual growth, it is especially helpful as a taster for those thinking about further counselling training.

We run the course several times a year at Waverley Abbey House, and this November, the course will be running at Pilgrim Hall in East Sussex. As well as benefiting from the IBCC teaching, enjoy times of spiritual refreshment in the beautiful and peaceful surroundings of one of these two houses. We look forward to welcoming you.

**Upcoming dates:**
19-23 November 2012, 10-14 June 2013
at Pilgrim Hall
18-22 March, 12-16 August and 18-22
November 2013 at Waverley Abbey House

For more information/to apply, visit
**www.cwr.org/uk/training**
or call **+44 (0)1252 784719**.

# After the avalanche

**FOR READING & MEDITATION - JOB 1:1-22**

'In all this, Job did not sin by charging God with wrongdoing.' (v.22)

**A**nother form of darkness in which we sometimes find ourselves engulfed is that of suffering and pain. It is at this point that the faith of many experiences its deepest shocks. A woman writes, 'My sister was a very godly woman but she suffered so dreadfully in childbirth. Why didn't God spare her this suffering since she was such a godly woman?' A professor in a great Christian university in the United States of America was hit by a truck, knocked down and suffered a broken leg. After he recovered, he told the students in the morning chapel, 'I no longer believe in a personal God. If there were a personal God, would He not have whispered to me to beware of the danger of the coming truck and have saved me from this calamity?' The professor was struck and in his fall his faith crashed too.

**FURTHER STUDY**

Job 2:1-10;
James 5:7-11

1. How did Job sum up our human experience?
2. What does James say of Job?

Can God hold us fast in such times? Can we find treasures in this darkness, too? With all my heart I say – we can. The ancient patriarch Job wrote more than patronising platitudes about suffering: he'd been there and back. He could describe intense suffering in the first person because of his own sea of pain. Blameless, upright, clean-living and respected by everyone – God included – he experienced a wave of calamity that almost blotted him out. He lost his livestock, crops, land, servants, and every one of his ten children. Soon after that he lost his health, his last human hope of earning a living. How did he react to all this? Well, you read his response in the words of our text for today.

Right now I'm shaking my head with amazement as I consider his words. Would you have responded in such a way? Would I? I wonder.

**O Father, is it possible that You can give us such grace at such a moment? It is written in Your Word, so I must believe it. Give me Job's secret so that I, too, might respond to all suffering with grace and not a grudge. In Jesus' name. Amen.**

# A recipe for handling problems

## FOR READING & MEDITATION - JOB 42:1-17

'I know that you can do all things ... Surely I spoke of things
I did not understand ...' (vv.2-3)

**W**e looked yesterday at the darkness which engulfed
God's servant Job and today we ask ourselves: how
could he go through all that and not rail against the
Almighty? Just think of it – bankruptcy, pain, ten fresh
graves – yet we read that he worshipped God. He did not
sin, nor did he blame his Maker. The question raises itself
to almost cosmic proportions: why? Why could he ward off
bitterness and still maintain his faith?

I think one reason was because Job looked *up* and
accepted the fact of God's sovereignty. He sincerely
believed that the God who gave had every right to
take away. He had no arguments over God's rule
in his life and believed that God's sovereignty was
laced with love. Another reason was because he
counted on the promise of resurrection: 'I know
that my Redeemer lives, and that in the end ... I
will see God' (Job 19:25–26). He not only looked up
– he looked *ahead*. He counted on God's promise
to make all things clear at the resurrection.
He knew that at that time all pain, death and
sorrow would be removed. Job endured the day-
to-day happenings in the light of the next day's
envisioning. A further reason was because he looked *within*
and confessed his own lack of understanding. Our text for
today puts this point most effectively. Job confessed his
inability to put it all together and did not feel compelled to
know just why God allowed things to happen to him in the
way they did. God was the judge: that was fine with Job.

That was how Job picked up the pieces after the avalanche
had struck. It takes a firm faith to respond like that, but
the fact that Job did it shows it can be done.

### FURTHER STUDY

Psa. 121:1-8;
2 Cor. 4:16-18;
Heb. 12:1-3

1. Where should we look when in difficulties?

2. What are we to throw off?

O God, how I long to respond to the problems in my world in the
way Job responded to his. Help me to begin to practise these
principles today and then go on to master them in the weeks that
lie ahead. For Your own dear name's sake. Amen.

# The inevitability of suffering

**FOR READING & MEDITATION - JOB 5:1-18**

'Yet man is born to trouble as surely as sparks fly upward.' (v.7)

**W**e continue meditating on the question of suffering and pain. It's surprising how many believe that God should spare good-living people from troubles. I have asked readers to imagine the following scenario before, but I believe it is helpful to repeat here. Suppose it could be guaranteed that disaster would always strike the wicked alone – what kind of world would it be? Its laws would always be in a process of suspension to accommodate the righteous. Gravity wouldn't pull you over a parapet even though you leaned out too far – provided, of course, you were a Christian. The universe would no longer be dependable, for in any situation involving another person you would never be sure which laws would act for you. Much would depend on the character of that other person – and that would only be clear after the event had taken place – one way or the other! Such a situation would be ridiculous.

**FURTHER STUDY**

Gen. 3:17-19;
James 4:1-3;
Rev. 21:1-5

1. Why is suffering inevitable?

2. Why is suffering not eternal?

I do not question that God can and sometimes does intervene and save His children in particular situations, for one thing is sure – you cannot put God into a straitjacket in His own universe. The laws He has designed for the running of the universe are His habitual way of maintaining it, but He is perfectly capable of suspending those laws when He sees fit. Such an event we call a miracle. But miracles, by definition, cannot be the norm.

When Jesus hung upon the cross, the crowd cried, 'He trusts in God. Let God rescue him' (Matt. 27:43). God did not rescue Him; *He did something better.* And it is along this line of the 'something better' that we must search for the Christian solution to the problem of suffering.

**Father, I realise that I am looking into the heart of one of the deepest mysteries of the universe - suffering and pain. Help me to believe that when You don't deliver me it is because You have something better. Amen.**

# God has suffered too

FOR READING & MEDITATION - ISAIAH 53:1-12

'Surely he took up our infirmities and carried our sorrows ...' (v.4)

**W**hen all human attempts to relieve suffering and pain do not work and even prayer seems not to prevail – what then? Though there may be no miracle of deliverance, can we believe that God is still at work and is with us in the suffering and pain? God did not rescue Christ from the sufferings of the cross, because it was only through those sufferings that His perfect purposes could be achieved. The key, I believe, is this – *God only allows what He can use.*

Christianity is the only religion in the world that dares to ask its followers to believe that God can work through suffering and pain, because it is the only religion that can say its God has suffered too. How much has God suffered? Some think He suffered only during the hours that Christ hung upon the cross, but there is much more to it than that. Jesus was the 'Lamb that was slain from the creation of the world' (Rev. 13:8). Can you see what that means? Ages before the cross was set up on Calvary, there was a cross in the heart of God. The piercing pain of Calvary went through the heart of the Almighty the moment He laid the foundations of the world. Throughout the long millennia of history God carried with Him the pain of being parted from His only begotten Son. Then came the awful moment when it happened on Calvary. And was that the end of God's sufferings? No, now His sufferings continue in the world's rejection of His Son and, at times, in the indifference of some of His children – you and me.

Doesn't it mean something, even everything, to know that though living in this world costs us suffering and pain, it costs God more? I find this thought deeply comforting, and challenging. I pray that you will too.

**FURTHER STUDY**

Gen. 6:5-6;
1 Peter 2:18-25

1. Why is God invincible but not invulnerable?

2. What is God's example for us?

**O Father, my suffering seems so small when placed against the suffering You must have experienced in the giving of Your only Son. You turned your pains to good account; help me to do the same. In Jesus' name I ask it. Amen.**

# A priceless treasure

**FOR READING & MEDITATION - 2 CORINTHIANS 1:1-11**

'Praise be to ... the God of all comfort, who comforts us in all our troubles, so that we can comfort...' (vv.3-4)

**O**f all the letters Paul wrote, his second letter to the Corinthians is regarded as the most autobiographical. In it the great apostle lifts the curtain that hung over his private life and allows us to catch a glimpse of his human frailties and needs. You really need to read the whole letter in one sitting to catch the emotion that moves and surges through Paul's soul. It is in this letter that he records the specifics of his anguish, tears, afflictions, satanic opposition, beatings, loneliness, imprisonment, hunger, shipwrecks, sleepless nights and so on. And what came out of it all? What were the treasures that were discovered in the darkness?

**FURTHER STUDY**

2 Cor. 7:6-7;
11:23-33

1. What kinds of suffering did Paul endure?

2. Where can we receive comfort?

One treasure is found in the word 'comfort'. The word appears again and again in the passage before us today. Because he had suffered, the apostle was able to enter into other people's problems with a capacity that he would never have had if he had not gone through those experiences. Have you noticed that when you have gone through a time of personal suffering and pain you are able to enter into other people's problems with more than a shallow pat on the back and a tired, 'May the Lord bless you'? Now you have genuine, in-depth understanding and empathy. And you perhaps understand how to comfort others because you yourself have received the comfort of God.

Are you suffering right now? Our loving heavenly Father is never preoccupied or removed when we are enduring sadness and affliction. He is there at your side this very moment. Let Him surround you with His special comfort and then, perhaps weeks or months later, you will be able to pass on that same powerful comfort to others.

**O God of all comfort, help me to be not only a receiver of comfort but also a giver of it. And Father, if I can unearth just this one treasure from the darkness of suffering and pain, then I will be rich indeed. In Jesus' name. Amen.**

# Shattered hopes and plans

**FOR READING & MEDITATION - LUKE 8:26-39**
'Then all the people ... asked Jesus to leave them,
because they were overcome with fear.' (v.37)

**W**e continue exploring the fact that we can discover hidden treasures in the darkness that we could never discover in the light. Another form of darkness in which God invites us to take the torch of faith and look for meaning is the darkness of shattered hopes and plans. I have no doubt that many reading these lines are there right now. The time when all our plans seem to go wrong is one of the most difficult periods of life. It throws confusion into everything, for so much can be geared to those plans. But listen carefully to me – there are treasures to be found even in this deep darkness.

Look with me at how Jesus reacted to the obstructing of His plans in the incident that is before us today. After He had healed the man possessed by demons, the people came to see what had happened and found the man 'sitting at Jesus' feet, dressed and in his right mind' (v.35). The passage goes on to say, 'and they were afraid'. Afraid of what? They were afraid of something they could not understand. They could handle insanity better than they could handle sanity. Insanity was familiar to them, but the deliverance of the demonic was something very unfamiliar. So they begged Jesus to leave.

**FURTHER STUDY**

Ruth 1:1-22

1. How were Naomi's hopes shattered?

2. Contrast the attitudes of Orpah and Ruth.

How did Jesus react to this apparent blocking of His ministry in that region? He turned in another direction, and when you read the next two chapters you find one astonishing miracle after another. He turned the blocking into a blessing. If He couldn't do this, He could do that. The frustration turned to fruitfulness. So when your plans are upset, do what Jesus did – utilise the grace that flows from God and prepare to turn in another direction.

**Father, help me not to be deterred by the blocking of my plans. Give me a resilient spirit to forget the broken plans and by Your grace make new and better ones. In Jesus' name I ask it. Amen.**

# 8 DEC Isolation becomes revelation

**FOR READING & MEDITATION – REVELATION 1:4-20**

'I, John ... was on the island of Patmos because of the word of God
and the testimony of Jesus.' (v.9)

**Y**esterday we saw how opposition did not deter Jesus but
deflected Him, and resulted in a series of astonishing
miracles: the deflection became a spur. There are treasures
to be found in every difficulty, a dawn in every midnight,
opportunities in every opposition. I know I am talking
to someone now whose plans have been completely
overturned. Maybe you are sitting reading these lines
feeling as if the world has caved in on you. May I encourage
you to lift up your heart – the eternal God has a word for
you. His grace and power are flowing towards you at this

**FURTHER
STUDY**

Ruth 2:1-22

1. Why did Boaz
praise Ruth?

2. What did
Naomi come
to realise?

very moment and, if you are open to receive,
the block can become a blessing, the frustration
can be turned into fruitfulness, and the setback
become a stepping stone.

When John found himself on the Isle of Patmos,
incarcerated for the sake of the gospel, it must
have seemed that his ministry and all his plans
had been rudely shattered. He says, 'I John ... was
on the island called Patmos because of God's Word,
the witness of Jesus' (1:9, *The Message*). However,

he continues, 'It was Sunday and I was in the Spirit,
praying. I heard a loud voice ... "Write what you see ..."'
(vv.10–11). Isolated, and prevented from preaching the
gospel, he wrote a book that has blessed men and women
down the centuries. The place of isolation became a place
of revelation.

This is what can happen to you today if you do not
allow yourself to sink into the depths of darkness and
instead receive the grace that God is offering to you now.
Sit down amongst your broken and shattered plans and
'write out' the vision of the new and better ones that God
will give you.

**Lord Jesus, strengthen me and guide me to 'write out' my personal
vision of Your coming victory. Help me to see that the break up
of present plans can lead to bigger and better ones. For Your own
dear name's sake I pray. Amen.**

# Working with a wound

SUN
**9 DEC**

**FOR READING & MEDITATION - MATTHEW 14:1-14**

'When Jesus heard what had happened, he withdrew by boat
privately ... the crowds followed him ...' (v.13)

**W**e continue focusing on the thought that when our
present plans are shattered, God can enable us to
build bigger and better ones. But remember that this
treasure comes only to those who search for meaning and
understanding.

Consider the picture before us today. Jesus had just heard
that John the Baptist, his relative and forerunner, had been
beheaded. The account says, 'When Jesus got the news,
he slipped away by boat to an out-of-the-way place by
himself' (v.13, *The Message*). No doubt the Saviour longed
to be alone with His grief, but verse 13 continues,
'But unsuccessfully ... Soon a lot of people from the
nearby villages walked around the lake to where he
was.' They broke up His plans. Now what did Jesus
do? Did He turn on the people and reprimand them
for invading His privacy? Listen again to what the
account says: 'When he saw them coming, he was
overcome with pity and healed their sick' (v.14,
*The Message*). He turned His hurt into healing and
responded to the situation with infinite tenderness
and compassion. Jesus had a wound in His heart,
but that wound became healing for others.

Now you may think that it is insensitive of me
to talk about ministry to others when you are
hurting, but I believe it is important for us to understand
these things if we are to leave behind self-pity and move
in a new direction. We do not need to 'have it all together'
to be a blessing. Our wounds can become healing for
others. The same Jesus who ministered with a wound in
His heart can both minister to you and through you. Oh,
I pray that you may feel His touch at this very moment –
this very hour.

**FURTHER STUDY**

Ruth 2:23-3:18

1. How did Ruth minister to others even though she was a widow?

2. Compare Boaz and Ruth to Jesus and you.

**Blessed Lord Jesus, I am comforted to know that You too must
have winced when wounded, but You used your wounds to reach out
to others. Now let Your wounds heal my wounds and my wounds
heal someone else's. For Your own dear name's sake. Amen.**

# 'The show will go on'

**FOR READING & MEDITATION – PSALM 62:1-12**
'He alone is my rock and my salvation; he is my fortress,
I shall never be shaken.' (v.2)

We are discovering that there are treasures to be found in every period of darkness – even the darkness of shattered hopes and plans. Someone has spoken of 'getting meaning out of life's remainders'. Sometimes life leaves us with nothing but 'remainders'. Everything we longed for has gone and we are left with nothing more than reminders of what might have been. But what I am saying is this – we can discover meaning from those 'remainders'. It was Franklin D. Roosevelt who said, 'When you get to the end of your rope, tie a knot and hang on'. Are you at the end of a rope at this moment? Then take his advice – tie a knot and hang on.

**FURTHER STUDY**

Ruth 4:1-13;
Eph. 2:11-13,19

1. How did God change the scenery in Ruth's life for blessing?

2. Compare Ruth to Gentile Christians.

There is a passage in the book of Revelation that says, '... there was silence in heaven for about half an hour' (Rev. 8:1). I heard a preacher say, 'That was because God was moving the scenery for the next act.' Can you dare believe that in the period when important plans have broken up, God is at work moving the scenery for the next act? Hold steady – the show will go on. In the meantime, prepare to let God give you the assurance that there is a point and a purpose to what has happened to you. Let the 'remainders' be your reminders that with God all things are possible.

I met a man some time ago who told me that a year earlier his plans to emigrate and start a new life with his family had been overturned just days before he was due to leave the country. 'I thought life had come to an end,' he told me, 'but within weeks God moved me into an exciting new career that hitherto I could not have dreamed was possible.' The upset served only to set him up.

**O Father, drive the truth deeply into my spirit that there are treasures to be found in every darkness. Show me how to take the torch of faith and look for meaning in every perplexing situation. This I ask in Christ's all-prevailing name. Amen.**

# The hidden 'better'

**FOR READING & MEDITATION - JOHN 16:5-16**

'In a little while you will see me no more, and then after a little while you will see me.' (v.16)

**H**ow it must have upset the plans of the disciples when they were told by Jesus that He was about to leave them! After three years it seemed His ministry was just beginning to make its mark and their hearts must have sunk within them as they heard Him say, 'I am soon about to leave you.' What a sense of spiritual loss must have stolen across their hearts: they would be left alone in the world without Him. Those disciples, remember, had given up their jobs to travel with Him. Peter had turned from his fishing nets, Matthew from his tax collecting, and so on. Jesus' announcement that He was soon to go away must have sounded like a thunder clap in their souls. It was the collapse of all their hopes and expectations.

However, His going brought them an even greater blessing. Our text puts it most beautifully when it says, 'It is for your good that I am going away' (v.7). In effect, Jesus was saying something like this, 'I will take away My physical presence, but instead you will experience My omnipresence. I will be closer to you than I have ever been before. The Holy Spirit will bring Me back, not just to be alongside, but within you. You will just have to drop into the recesses of your own heart and I will be there, burning bright and ready to bless.'

The disciples were to learn, as you and I must learn, that God never takes away the good unless He plans to replace it with the better. After Pentecost, the disciples must have said to each other, 'It is true He has gone, but somehow He is closer to us than ever.' Oh, if only we could learn that the shattering of our plans is but the prelude to the advancement of His!

## FURTHER STUDY

Ruth 4:13-21;
1 Pet. 2:9

1. How may aliens and commoners become royal people?

2. Contrast Naomi in Ruth 1:11-21 with Ruth 4:14-17.

O Father, when some 'good' is taken away and I am left feeling bereft, help me believe for the hidden 'better' that may be just round the corner. This I ask in Christ's peerless and precious name. Amen.

# When money takes wings

**FOR READING & MEDITATION - PROVERBS 23:1-8**

'Cast but a glance at riches, and they are gone, for they will surely sprout wings ...' (v.5)

**T**oday we focus on another form of darkness – the darkness of financial failure or material loss. Dare we believe that God can help us find treasure when there has been a financial catastrophe? Well, once again I say – He can!

Many years ago I had a friend who suffered a serious financial reverse and lost everything – literally everything. He came out of it, however, with a philosophy of life that enabled him to say, 'Never again will I be broken by material loss.' And why? Because out of his downfall he built a

**FURTHER STUDY**

Mark 4:13-20; James 5:1-6

1. Why are riches deceitful?

2. Why may rich people be poor?

biblical framework which enabled him to see the whole issue of finance from God's perspective. He has come back now from bankruptcy and is once again a wealthy man, but this time around he holds his possessions more loosely and sees himself, not as a proprietor, but as a steward. You see, it sometimes takes an upset to set us up, in the sense that we do not gain the right perspective on things until we are brought down into a crisis.

Do you find yourself this moment in a financial reverse? Have you been stripped of many, if not all, your assets? Then follow me carefully over the next few days, for I want to share with you some principles that will help to rebuild your life and bring you into a deeper understanding than ever before of the biblical purpose of possessions. This also applies to those who may not at this moment be in reduced financial circumstances, because, in a world such as this, a financial reverse can come at any time. It behoves us all to learn how to live independently of our possessions, because one day we may be called upon to do just that.

**Father, help me, once and for all, to settle my attitude to my possessions. I know I can never be a true disciple of Yours until I see my discipleship in terms, not of what I own, but of what I owe. Help me, dear Father. Amen.**

# Transferring ownership

**FOR READING & MEDITATION - GENESIS 22:1-19**

'... because you have done this and have not withheld your son,
your only son, I will surely bless you ...' (vv.16-17)

The first thing we must get straight about the whole issue of money and possessions is that in themselves they are not evil. Some Christians speak scathingly of those who have a good deal of money. The Bible never does that. It brings to task those who make money their god, but it never rails against money as such. So, see clearly that money in itself is not evil; it lends itself to a thousand philanthropies, feeds the hungry, clothes the naked, succours the destitute, and through it many errands of mercy are performed. It is true that money cannot bring happiness, but as someone said, 'It can certainly put our creditors in a better frame of mind'.

Whether you have a little or a lot of this world's goods, I suggest that if you have never taken the following step, you do it now – *in a definite act of commitment, transfer the ownership of all your possessions into the hands of God.* Those of you who have been stripped of everything will need to do this as an act of faith, indicating that should God allow you to have possessions again, you will see yourself as a steward and not a proprietor. The friend to whom I referred yesterday – the one who lost everything – told me that after reading the passage which is before us today, he got on his knees and by faith said to God, 'Whatever comes into my hands again, I will hold in trust for You.' That act of dedication becomes the point of transformation. God took him at his word and helped him rebuild his life.

If in reality we do not own anything, but are given things from God, then the commonsense thing is to say, 'Lord, I'm not the owner, but the ower.' We must never forget that.

**FURTHER STUDY**

1 Chron. 29:1-16

1. How did David view his wealth?

2. How did people give to the work of God?

**Father, so often I am afraid to follow You all the way. Give me the faith of Abraham to believe that all things are in Your hands. Right now I lay everything I own on Your altar. It's no longer mine; it's Yours. Amen.**

# Hitched to a plough

**FOR READING & MEDITATION - COLOSSIANS 3:1-17**

'Set your minds on things above, not on earthly things.' (v.2)

**O**nce we have transferred ownership of all our possessions and material assets to God – what then? Next we need to *streamline our lives for the purposes of God's kingdom.* David Livingstone once said, 'I will place no value on anything that I have or possess except in relation to the Kingdom of Christ. If anything I have will advance that Kingdom, it shall be given or kept, whichever will best promote the glory of Him to whom I owe all my hopes, both for time and eternity.'

Commenting on Livingstone's words, one writer said, 'That first sentence of Livingstone's should become the life motto of every Christian. Each of us should repeat it slowly to ourselves every day, "I will place no value on anything I have or possess except in relation to the Kingdom of Christ."' If it advances the kingdom it has value – if it is useless to the kingdom it is valueless.

**FURTHER STUDY**

Exod. 36:1-7;
2 Cor. 8:1-5

1. What problem faced Moses when building God's house?

2. What was remarkable about the Macedonian churches?

In the days when missionaries were able to work in China, John Wanamaker, a Christian businessman, who visited that country in order to see that the donations of people were being used wisely and to the best advantage, tells this story. One day he came to a village where there was a beautiful little church. In a nearby field he caught sight of a young man yoked to an ox, ploughing a field. He went over and asked the reason for this strange sight. An old man who was guiding the plough from behind said, 'When we were trying to build our church, my son and I had no money to give. My son said, "Let us sell one of our two oxen and I will take its yoke." We did so and were able to give the money we made towards the building of the church.' Wanamaker wept!

**Father, perhaps I should be weeping, too, but for a different reason – weeping when I ask myself how much of my life is streamlined for kingdom purposes. Would I be willing to be yoked to a plough? Help me, dear Father. In Jesus' name. Amen.**

# 'Above all distinctions'

**FOR READING & MEDITATION - PHILIPPIANS 4:4-13**

'I have learned the secret of being content in any and every
situation ... in plenty or in want.' (v.12)

A third principle of rebuilding after a financial
catastrophe is this – *learn what it means to be free to
use either poverty or plenty*. History shows that as a rule
people try to defend themselves against financial disaster
in one of two ways. One is by saving as much as possible,
and the other is by renouncing all interest in money or
material things. If, in building up financial reserves,
people allow their trust and confidence to be focused on
amassing riches and material possessions rather than on
God, they become as metallic as the coins they seek. They
are in bondage to material gain. But the other type
can be in bondage too, for washing one's hands of
material things shows a bondage, not to riches,
but to poverty.

The person who is only free to use plenty is
bound by that, and the person who is only free to
use poverty is bound by that. Both are in bondage.
But the person who, like Paul in the text before
us today, has learned the secret of being content
whether living in plenty or in want, experiences
a true freedom.

I remember reading the story of a missionary in
India who got into conversation with a high caste
Indian at a remote railway station. 'Are you travelling
on the next train?' asked the missionary. 'No,' replied the
Indian, 'the train has only third class carriages. It's all
right for you, because you are a Christian and you are
above such distinctions.'

'Above such distinctions' – that is true Christian living.
Third class doesn't degrade us and first class doesn't exalt
us. Hallelujah!

**FURTHER STUDY**

Prov. 11:24-28;
1 Tim. 6:6-19;
Heb. 13:5

1. Why do
some people
experience
many griefs?

2. What should
rich people do?

**Loving heavenly Father, help me to know what it is to be free -
really free. Save me from being entangled by plenty or broken
by poverty. Do for me what You did for the great apostle Paul. In
Jesus' name I ask it. Amen.**

# Staying on course

**FOR READING & MEDITATION – 2 CORINTHIANS 1:12-23**

'... we have conducted ourselves in the world ... not according to
worldly wisdom but according to God's grace.' (v.12)

**W**e look at one more principle which can help us rebuild
our lives when overtaken by a financial disaster –
*learn to differentiate between a need and a want.* But what
are needs? And how do we differentiate between our needs,
and our wants and desires? Someone has defined a need
like this: 'We need as much as will make us physically,
mentally and spiritually fit for the purposes of God, and
anything beyond that belongs to the needs of others.' If
this is true, then how do we decide what belongs to our
needs and what belongs to the needs of others? I wish I
could answer that, but it is a matter that each of
us must work out between ourselves and God.
Go over your life in God's presence and see what
belongs to your needs and what really comes
under the category of wants.

**FURTHER
STUDY**

Matt. 6:19-24;
Luke 12:13-21

1. How can we
ensure money
serves us
instead of us
serving it?

2. Why was the
rich man a fool?

'But,' someone may say, 'what about luxuries
– things we don't really need but which make
life more pleasant?' Again, these things are to be
worked out in prayer between yourself and God.
Only the Holy Spirit can sensitise our consciences
and tune us to His purposes for our lives, and each
of us may come out with different conclusions.

A fisherman said, 'Some time ago I was on a
lake. I pulled in my oars and let the boat drift. As I looked
at the surrounding water I could see no drift at all, and only
as I looked at a fixed point on the shore could I see how far
I was drifting.' The story is a parable. If you look around
to see what others are doing and merely follow them, you
will have no sense of drift. Only as you keep your eyes on
Jesus and remain fixed on Him will you know whether you
are staying on God's course – or drifting from it.

**Gracious Father, sensitise my inner being so that I hear Your voice
in everything I do. Teach me what belongs to my needs and what
belongs to the needs of others. In Jesus' name I pray. Amen.**

# 'More to follow'

**FOR READING & MEDITATION – 2 CORINTHIANS 9:1-15**

'And God is able to make all grace abound to you ...' (v.8)

**W**e move on now to consider a form of darkness that can be filled with deep pain and sadness – the darkness of broken relationships. I doubt whether there is anyone reading these lines who has not in one way or another experienced the hurt that comes from a difficult or broken relationship. At this very moment some of you will be going through such an experience, perhaps the discovery of infidelity by a marriage partner, or a separation, a divorce, a rift between parents and children, or a broken engagement or friendship. Out of loyalty to their families, many face the world with a smile, but inwardly they are torn and wounded.

Whatever the specifics of the situation, any rift in a relationship can be a deeply wounding experience. Are there treasures to be found in the darkness of a broken relationship? If you are in this kind of situation at present, it may be difficult for you to believe that you can come through stronger spiritually, but I want to assure you that you can. A little patient searching in the darkness that surrounds you can yield the most priceless treasures.

'How?' I hear you ask – 'How?' First, remind yourself that God provides sufficient grace and strength for us to deal with every situation that comes our way. You are not the first to be in this situation; others have been there and have proved that God gives grace upon grace. An anonymous donor sent a poor man a £5 note every week with the message, 'This is yours; use it wisely, there is more to follow.' God does something similar with His grace. Every time you receive it there is always a note attached that says, 'more to follow'.

**FURTHER STUDY**

Psa. 55:4-14;
Heb. 4:14-16

1. What could David not endure?

2. What should we do in times of need?

**Father, help me see that You do not just supply me with grace; You overwhelm me with it. Help me to be a living illustration of the truth that You give grace upon grace. In Jesus' name I ask it. Amen.**

# A searching question

**FOR READING & MEDITATION - PSALM 139:13-24**
'See if there is any offensive way in me, and lead me in
the way everlasting.' (v.24)

**W**e continue taking up the torch of faith to explore
some of the treasures that are to be found in the
darkness of broken relationships. Keep in mind that these
treasures are only found as you seek them out. They don't
just appear out of nowhere; they have to be searched for –
with diligence, patience and trust.

Reminding yourself to rest in the truth that God provides
'grace upon grace', you should then face this question
with courage and determination: 'How much may I have
contributed to the problem?' In the midst of your pain,
this might be a difficult thing for you even to
consider, and if you can't, don't worry – when the
pain subsides you can come back to this question.
But whether you do it now or later, keep in mind
that face it you must. Our tendency whenever we
are hurt is to see ourselves as a victim and forget
that we may have contributed in some way to the
problem. It may well be that you are an innocent
victim, but be ready and willing, nevertheless, to
see if there is any way in which you may have
contributed to the difficulties.

If, in looking at yourself, you find there are
things that you are responsible for, confess these
things to God and ask His forgiveness. This action
will help you make a clearer and more objective
assessment of the situation. Now, if you discover that you
have hurt others, don't go running to them right away
to ask for their forgiveness. You will need to know God's
timing in this. It is always right to ask forgiveness of those
we have hurt, but if it is not done at the right time it can
create a wrong impression – they may, for example, feel
that you are doing it to gain an advantage over them.

**FURTHER
STUDY**

Matt. 5:21-26;
Jer. 17:9-10

1. Why do we
need to allow
God to search
our hearts?

2. What may
be more
important than
worshipping
God?

**Father, I see that right motives and right actions are not always
enough; right actions must be done at the right time. Help me to
grasp this lesson, for I see that a mistimed word can hinder rather
than help. In Jesus' name I pray. Amen.**

# NEXT ISSUE

# Walking Free

Start the New Year with a fresh look at God's wonderful provision of grace, and how receiving it enables us to thrive spiritually.

In the next issue, Selwyn invites us to live in the fullness and freedom of grace, allowing it to energise our walk along the road of discipleship. Learn to become an example for those around you as you:

- ask for the grace we need
- appreciate what grace cost Jesus
- pass grace on to others.

Step into 2013 with renewed thankfulness to God and confidence in what He wants to do in and through you.

**Every Day with Jesus**
JAN/FEB 2013

## Walking Free

'... [God] has saved us and called us to a holy life – not because of anything we have done but because of his own purpose and grace.'
2 Timothy 1:9

Daily devotional written by Selwyn Hughes      **CWR**

**Also available as ebook/ esubscription**

OBTAIN YOUR COPY FROM
**CWR, a Christian bookshop or National Distributor.**
If you would like to take out a subscription, see the order form at the back of these notes. Please note that from the Jan/Feb 2013 issue, the price will increase to £2.95 per issue.

# In whom do we trust?

**FOR READING & MEDITATION – PSALM 56:1-13**
'When I am afraid, I will trust in you.' (v.3)

I hope you were able to see the point and purpose of what I said yesterday. If we go *at the wrong time* to ask forgiveness of someone for something we have done, the action can hinder rather than help the situation.

A woman whose husband left her took the first two steps I have suggested: first, she reminded herself that God was with her and, second, she faced with great courage the possibility that in some way she may have contributed to the problem. She asked God for His forgiveness and then immediately went searching for her husband to ask for his forgiveness. He interpreted this as manipulation and was not ready to receive it. Instead of drawing him to her, it drove him further away. We must be strong enough and trustful enough to await God's timing in all situations.

**FURTHER STUDY**

Psa. 20:1-9;
Isa. 31:1-3; 36:6

1. Where do some people put their trust?

2. What happens when our trust is placed in others?

This brings me to my next suggestion – learn how to become a truly secure person. The secret of living successfully in this world is to remember that we are designed by God to draw our security as persons primarily from Him and not from our earthly relationships. Most of us get this wrong and draw our life from our horizontal relationships – the people around us, family, friends and so on – rather than from our vertical relationship with God. And we never know how flimsy that vertical relationship is until the horizontal relationships in which we are involved fall apart. Many have told me that they never realised how dependent they were on others until the others were no longer there; then they were devastated. We are to enter into earthly relationships and enjoy them, but we are never to be dependent on them for our life. We are to be dependent only on God.

**O Father, I see that when I draw my life from earthly relationships, then when they fail my life seems over. But when I draw my life from You, then life can never fail – for You are unchanging and unfailing. Thank You, my Father. Amen.**

# In God we trust

**FOR READING & MEDITATION - PSALM 91:1-16**

'He who dwells in the shelter of the Most High ... will say ...
"He is my refuge and my fortress ..."' (vv.1-2)

If there is one thing that is clear about the whole area of
relationships it is this – relationships can hurt. A friend
of mine says, 'God calls us to relate to people who are
guaranteed to hurt us and fail us.' This is why we must
find a source of security that is not in people, but in God,
the unfailing One. This does not mean we must withdraw
from people, but that we do not use them as the source
of our life. Once we see that God, and God alone, is our
true security, then, when earthly relationships fail, we are
shaken but not shattered. There is a five foot drop and not
a thousand foot drop.

Let me tell you how secure people will behave
when engulfed in the darkness of broken
relationships. Having reminded themselves that
God's grace is ever-sufficient, and having looked
at any way in which they may have contributed
to the difficulty, and thrown themselves in
utter dependency upon God, they will be strong
enough to sit back and wait for God to show them
exactly what to do. They will not act precipitately
because they are no longer dependent on their
earthly relationships to hold them together, but
are dependent on God. They will move with
poise and prayerful determination into the situation. They
know that there is no guarantee that poise and prayerful
determination will bring about a resolution of the problem
but, having done what God wants them to do, they are able
to relax and leave the outcome to Him.

Once you have moved your point of dependency from
the horizontal to the vertical, and are following God's
direction and guidance in all things, then, though you may
still hurt, you will not be destroyed.

## FURTHER STUDY

Psa. 3:1-8;
118:1-9

1. Why could
the psalmist
be peaceful in
adversity?

2. How did the
Lord answer
the psalmist?

**O Father, I am so thankful that there is a way to live which
guarantees, not that I will never be hurt, but that I will never be
destroyed. Help me embrace that. In Jesus' name I pray. Amen.**

# The priceless pearl

**FOR READING & MEDITATION - PSALM 112:1-10**
'Even in darkness light dawns for the upright ...' (v.4)

**O**nce we settle for the truth that when we draw our security directly from Jesus, and not from our earthly relationships, we may still get hurt but not destroyed – then we have discovered one of the most priceless treasures in the universe. Unfortunately, many do not find this treasure except in the darkness of broken relationships. Like Isaiah, they do not see the glory and sufficiency of the One on the throne until they go through an experience that seems like death. 'In the year that King Uzziah died, I saw the Lord ...' (Isa. 6:1).

**FURTHER STUDY**

Job 28:1-10;
Matt. 13:44-45;
Heb. 12:14-15

1. What must we do to obtain God's treasures?

2. What must we be careful not to miss?

Some broken relationships can be healed, but some cannot. Our part is to ensure that we do everything we can to restore them and then leave the matter in God's hands. If restoration comes, then fine, but if not, providing we are open all the time to doing what God wants us to do, then God will continue to bless us, even though the relationship is not restored.

I know many Christians who are caught up at this very moment in broken relationships and unhappy home situations and I observe them day by day doing what the oyster does when it gets an irritating grain of sand in its shell – they form a pearl around the problem. Just as the oyster down there in the darkness of the ocean builds a pearl around an irritant, so will God enable you to throw around all your difficult situations, especially broken relationships, a priceless pearl of character. The darkness then becomes a trusting place where daily you and God work things out in ways that glorify His name. And had the darkness not come, you might never have discovered the treasure.

**O Father, I see so clearly that I am not motivated to dig for treasure until I am engulfed by darkness. But the treasures I can find there are worth much more than they cost. Help me to believe that, not just with my head, but with my heart. Amen.**

**FOR READING & MEDITATION - LUKE 2:21-35**

'And a sword will pierce your own soul too.' (v.35)

**W**e focus now, in the period leading up to Christmas Day, on a type of darkness which engulfs many at this time of the year – the darkness of depression. Statistics suggest that more people get depressed at Christmas than at any other time of the year. It is also the time when there is often seen a peak in the number of people who harm themselves. These figures have given rise to the term 'Christmas depression'. Can we find treasure in this type of darkness? Once again, I hope to show you that we can!

In the passage before us today you will no doubt have noticed the strange and startling words with which Simeon ended his remarks to Mary, 'And a sword will pierce your own soul too.' I wonder what Mary thought of that deeply disturbing statement! One moment she was enjoying the thrill of holding the incarnate Son of God in her arms and the next moment she was told that as a result of His presence in the world a sword would pierce her soul. Simeon's prediction, I believe, had reference to such things as the flight into Egypt, the slaughter that would take place at Bethlehem, the later rejection of our Lord by His family and, above all, His crucifixion on the cross.

**FURTHER STUDY**

Psa. 42:1-10;
1 Pet. 5:7

1. What different emotions did the psalmist express?

2. What should we do when anxious?

But isn't it strange that the prediction made by Simeon to Mary seems to apply to millions of people the world over – the period surrounding Christ's birth seems to contain a sword that pierces their soul. Christmas may bring joy to some, but to others it brings gloom and sadness. The theatres may be full, the shops and streets be festooned with lights, the wine may flow fully and freely, but at the same time the hearts of multitudes are downcast and depressed. I wonder why?

**Father, help me come to grips with this issue, for I sense that in understanding what lies behind it I shall have a better idea of how to relate to others at Christmas, and be more sensitive to their deep inner needs. In Jesus' name. Amen.**

# 'It's Christmas – be happy'

**FOR READING & MEDITATION – PHILIPPIANS 2:1-11**

'Each of you should look not only to your own interests,
but also to the interests of others.' (v.4)

**W**e continue examining the question we raised yesterday: what is it about the birth of our Saviour that brings both joy and sorrow to the world? Why is it that at Christmas time some are prone to depression? One reason is because at Christmas people feel under pressure to 'be happy'. The expectation from almost everyone around is, 'This is Christmas – so drop all expressions of sadness and put on a happy face'. It reminds me of those experiences some children go through when they are taken to the seaside and told by their parents, 'Now we've brought you here to enjoy yourself, and enjoy yourself you will!' You see, those who are, for various reasons, feeling sad at Christmas and are under pressure from society not to show that sadness, may become resentful about this state of affairs and then push the resentment deep down inside them. And repressed resentment can soon turn into depression.

**FURTHER STUDY**

Acts 20:32-35;
1 Cor. 10:23-24;
Gal. 6:2

1. What principles of Christ did Paul remember?

2. What should we seek?

Psychologists Thomas Holmes and Richard Rahe produced an interesting scale of factors which lead to stress. They measured stress in terms of 'life change units'. On this scale, the death of a spouse rates 100 life-change units; divorce, 73 units; pregnancy, 40 units; change in living conditions, 25 units. *And Christmas rates 12 units.* His conclusion was that from a strictly human point of view, no one in their own strength can handle more than 300 units in a 12-month period without suffering physically or emotionally within the following two years. What does all this say to us? It says that we who are Christians need always to be sensitive to one another's circumstances and problems *but never so much as at Christmas.*

**O God, help me be aware! Help me to be sensitive to others' pain. Give me a heart that senses, understands and enters into the sorrows of others. May I not just bring the Christmas message but be it. In Jesus' name. Amen.**

# How much are you worth?

**FOR READING & MEDITATION - EPHESIANS 1:1-14**

'Praise be to ... God ... who has blessed us in the heavenly realms
with every spiritual blessing in Christ.' (v.3)

We saw yesterday that one of the contributing causes
of 'Christmas depression' is the expectation society
places upon people to 'be happy'. In some, this produces deep
resentment which, when repressed, turns into depression.

Another factor contributing to 'Christmas depression'
has to do with our faculty of memory. Our memories
are capable of remembering both good and bad things –
and either can trigger depression. A depressed teenager I
counselled one Christmas told me, 'My main memory of
Christmas is of my father coming home with a tree, but now
he is gone and will never do that for me again.' A
depressed woman, also suffering from 'Christmas
depression' said, 'My childhood Christmases had
so many disappointments and bad memories that
no matter how I try I can't enter into the spirit of
the season.' Two different memories, one good and
one bad, but each in its own way triggering the
same reaction.

**FURTHER STUDY**

Luke 12:22-31;
1 Pet. 1:18-21

1. Why are
we more
valuable than
all creation?

2. Why will our
salvation never
lose its value?

Yet another contributing factor of 'Christmas
depression' arises from the traditional receiving
and giving of gifts. How can receiving a gift
throw a person into darkness? Well, when some
people are given a valuable gift at Christmas
they interpret it as being more than they deserve, or, if
the gift is not valuable they interpret is as being less than
they deserve. It is not the gift, of course, that causes the
depression, but the person's perception of how the gift
relates to his or her worth. This is why the biggest barrier
against depression is to have a sense of worth that can
stand anything that happens to you – gain or loss, increase
or decrease, success or failure. And that comes only from
an understanding of how much you are worth to God.

**O Father, I see I need a sense of value that does not go up and
down with the kinds of gifts I receive at Christmas time. Give me,
therefore, a clear vision of how much I am worth to You. In Jesus'
name I ask it. Amen.**

# An important 'but'

**FOR READING & MEDITATION – JOHN 1:1-18**

'For the law was given through Moses; grace and truth came
through Jesus Christ.' (v.17)

**W**e pause on this Christmas Day to drink in again the
wonder of the incarnation. The text I have chosen for
today puts in one clear sentence the essential difference
between the Hebrew religion and Christianity. When we
speak of the Judaeo-Christian heritage and hyphenate
those two words, we must be clear what they mean. In
one sense, the Hebrew religion is the foundation on which
Christianity was built – the two faiths are continuous. In
another sense, however, they are discontinuous. There is a
break – a radical break. The New King James Version of the
verse before us today identifies that break by the
word 'but': 'For the law was given through Moses,
*but* grace and truth came through Jesus Christ.'

**FURTHER
STUDY**

Rom. 5:6-20;
8:1-4

1. Why was the
law powerless?

2. What has
grace achieved?

The Christian faith stands in contrast to the
basic precept of Judaism. Judaism says, 'The law
was given to Moses', that is, the word became
word. The word (the expression of God's thought)
was translated into another word – the Ten
Commandments. But Christianity says, 'Grace
and truth came through Jesus Christ.' Ah, that is
so different – now the Word becomes flesh.

The Jewish religion is built around a law; the Christian
religion is built around a Person. This is not a difference
in degree, it is a difference in kind. The end product is
different: one produced the Pharisee, correct, legal, proud,
separate; the other produced the Christian, humble,
receptive, loving, self-giving. The Jews say, 'We have a law';
Christians say, 'We have a Person' – and what a Person! The
babe wrapped in swaddling clothes and lying in a manger
is God. We gasp at such a revelation, but it's true. The Word
*has* become flesh. And that is the meaning of Christmas.

**Father, help me see that the Christian spirit is the Christmas
spirit extended through the whole year. Let the Christmas Word
show Himself through me. May I *be* the Christmas message. For
Your own dear name's sake. Amen.**

# 'Wounded healers'

**FOR READING & MEDITATION - PSALM 147:1-20**

'He heals the broken-hearted and binds up their wounds.' (v.3)

We return to the theme we were discussing in the days immediately prior to Christmas to ask ourselves: are there really treasures to be found in the darkness of depression? Yes, even this can yield its riches to those who are willing to search for meaning.

As a counsellor, it has been my privilege over the years to sit with hundreds of depressed people, and if there is one thing I have learned, it is this – in almost all cases, unless there is a chemical or biological cause, there comes a point when the depression lifts and goes away. Some experience the deep darkness of depression for days, others for weeks or even months, but eventually the sun breaks through again. Now here's my point: when it does, the personality seems to have a sensitivity to the needs and problems of others that is quite astonishing. Some of the greatest counsellors I have ever met are those who have struggled with and come through deep depression.

## FURTHER STUDY

Heb. 2:10-18;
4:14-15

1. What makes Christ a wonderful counsellor?

2. What does this mean for us?

For years now I have noticed something very interesting when I address groups of people on the subject of depression. If I am in a church and ask a general audience of people how many have suffered with depression, about 25 per cent of the congregation will raise their hands. In a training session for counsellors, the same question will bring a 90 per cent response. What does this say? It says that those who have struggled somehow become highly motivated to help others. It's one of the treasures that come out of the darkness – a deeper sensitivity and a more powerful motivation to reach out and heal the hurts of others. It is a fact that cannot be gainsaid – that often the best 'healers' are 'wounded healers'.

**My Father and my God, help me see that everything can be redeemed – even depression. I pray that I may do more than just experience sorrow – I may learn how to use it. In Jesus' name I pray. Amen.**

# The dynamics of confusion

**FOR READING & MEDITATION - JOB 12:13-25**

'He reveals the deep things of darkness and brings deep shadows into the light.' (v.22)

**W**e end our meditations on the theme *the treasures of darkness* by looking at a form of darkness into which almost every Christian is plunged at some time or other – the darkness of spiritual confusion.

Perhaps you are there at this moment. You thought you had things all figured out and you anticipated God moving in a certain direction, but suddenly He seems to have moved in an entirely different way than you expected – and now you are confused. None of us likes confusion because it makes us feel so utterly helpless and out of control. We feel better when we know how things will work out and just what we can expect in or from a certain situation. Let me assure you that the treasures that are to be found in the darkness of spiritual confusion are amongst the finest and most valuable we can ever discover.

**FURTHER STUDY**

2 Cor. 1:8-11; 4:7-18

1. What did Paul admit to?

2. How did he cope with confusion?

But before we look at some of those treasures, let's examine what I am going to call the dynamics of spiritual confusion. The unnerving thing about spiritual confusion is that it erodes our sense of competence. We all feel better when we know the outcome of any situation or when we can predict with some degree of certainty the way things will turn out. The trouble is, however, that although God tells us enough to establish, direct and nourish our faith, He doesn't always tell us enough to end confusion. I look back over my own Christian journey and can remember times, many times, when what God did and what He allowed seemed baffling, even maddening. Yet I know also that from those times I have unearthed treasures that are now worth more to me than the greatest riches on earth.

**O Father, whenever I am plunged into the darkness of spiritual confusion, help me dig for those treasures that are worth much more than they cost. Lord, I believe; help my unbelief. In Jesus' name. Amen.**

# Out of control

### FOR READING & MEDITATION - PSALM 125:1-5

'Those who trust in the LORD are like Mount Zion, which cannot
be shaken but endures for ever.' (v.1)

**W**hat is it about spiritual confusion that makes us feel
so uncomfortable? One reason is that it presents a
serious challenge to our desire to be in control.

Some time ago, when I was in the United States, the car
I had rented broke down on a deserted stretch of highway
between Akron, Ohio, and Washington. Although I got out
of my car, stood by the side of the road and tried to flag
down passers by, no one responded to my predicament. As
it grew dark, my anxiety level increased and I felt more
fearful, apprehensive and under threat than I had done
for years. I thought of all the American films I
had seen where people had been attacked when
stranded and, believe me, my prayers took on
an intensity that had not been there for some
time. There was some physical danger and some
inconvenience in that situation, but I remember
thinking that my high anxiety level suggested
that something more was going on inside me
than just that. Then it came to me – I was not in
control of the situation. I just didn't know what to
do or where to turn and I felt stupid, inadequate
and incompetent. My destiny was out of my
hands, even if only for a few hours, and I didn't
like the feeling.

**FURTHER STUDY**

Psa. 10:1-13;
Isa. 46:8-10

1. Why was
the psalmist
confused?

2. Why is our
perspective
limited but
God's limitless?

Confusion is an enemy to those who want to be in
control and, if we are honest, we will confess that most of
us experience some panic whenever we find ourselves in
a difficult situation where we are unable to take charge.
What does all this tell us? Doesn't it bring home to us the
solemn truth that, when it comes down to it, real trust is
more difficult than we thought?

**O God, I am so good at talking about trust, but so poor at actually
trusting. Forgive me for my desire to be always in control. Help
me to be a more trusting person. In Jesus' name I ask it. Amen.**

# Three popular strategies

### FOR READING & MEDITATION - ISAIAH 31:1-9

'Woe to those who go down to Egypt for help, who rely on horses ...
but do not ... seek help from the LORD.' (v.1)

L et me spell out three strategies that we use to cope
with the panicky feelings that come whenever we
are spiritually confused. One is to sidestep the feelings
altogether and deny that we are confused. Integrity
requires, however, that whatever is true must be looked at.
Pretence gets us nowhere but, I am afraid, it is a popular
strategy of many Christians. Don't run into denial, for
when you do, you are not being real.

Another strategy is to admit the confusion but
immediately go to work to replace it with some form of
understanding. I have often said to people in
counselling, 'Why do you think God has let this
happen?' only to hear an explanation that was so
unrelated to reality it was ridiculous. I wondered
for years why people did this and one day it hit
me – they were so disturbed by confusion that
they felt compelled to impose some 'order' on their
world by coming up with an explanation which,
although it really made no sense, was easier to
live with than the ambiguity and uncertainty of
confusion. They were not concerned about being
right; they were concerned about being in control. They
wanted to avoid the anxiety which came with the feeling
of helplessness. Clarity took precedence over accuracy.

**FURTHER
STUDY**

2 Chron. 20:1-15;
Zech. 4:6

1. What was
Jehoshaphat's
strategy?

2. How is God's
work achieved?

A third strategy that is used to reduce spiritual confusion
is to move into confusing situations with firm, positive
action and thus 'take charge'. Now some situations in life
have to be responded to in this way, but we must always
be sure that our firm and determined response to any
situation and our eagerness to 'take charge' spring, not
out of a desire to relieve discomfort, but out of a desire to
please God and do His perfect will.

**O God, I see yet again how prone I am to deal with my discomfort
in ways that point to the fact that I am not trusting You. Forgive
me and help me become a more dependent and trusting person.
For Your own dear name's sake. Amen.**

# 'As bad as that?'

## FOR READING & MEDITATION - PSALM 40:1-17

'Blessed is the man who makes the LORD his trust ...' (v.4)

**N**ow that we have seen something of the dynamics of confusion and the strategies we employ to cope with it, we ask ourselves, what are some of the treasures we can expect to find in the darkness of spiritual confusion? One such treasure is an increased sense of dependence on God.

All of us struggle with this issue of dependence, and those who say they don't are probably locked into denial. We find it difficult to rely totally on God. Although we lay great emphasis on trust in our hymns and songs and prayers, it's another matter when it comes down to doing it. A Christian couple who were being counselled by their minister heard him use these words, 'I rather think you have come to the position where you must trust God.' 'Oh dear,' they replied, without realising the import of the words they were using, 'has it got as bad as that?' It cuts across the grain of our human nature to be dependent on God to make our lives work; we feel utterly weak and helpless. We are afraid of *real* trust.

**FURTHER STUDY**

2 Tim. 1:7-12;
James 4:13-16

1. What was Paul convinced of?

2. Why will there always be some confusion in our lives?

Confusion is not as bad an experience as it might seem, for in the midst of it we become aware of our desire to be in control. We can then bring that in submission to God and experience a deeper sense of dependence than we have ever known before. God does enlighten us on certain points, but there are some levels of confusion that take a long time to disappear, and some may go on for a lifetime. At such times we can learn to relax and say to ourselves, 'With God in control, then I don't need answers. If He chooses to give them to me – fine; if not, that's fine too.' In such a climate, dependence not only survives – it thrives.

**O Father, bring me to a place in my Christian life where I can still go on even though I lack clear answers. I'm not there yet, but I'm growing. Take me further down this road, my Father. In Jesus' name I ask it. Amen.**

# Confidence in confusion

**FOR READING & MEDITATION - HABAKKUK 1:1-17**

'How long, O Lord, must I call for help, but you do not listen?' (v.2)

**W**e spend one final day looking at a typical treasure that can be discovered in the darkness of spiritual confusion – the treasure of a deeper dependence on God and a deeper trust in Him. It has been said that when life makes no sense, when moments of confusion shred our soul, there are three paths we can take: to abandon any claim to Christian belief and search for immediate relief and happiness; to run from confusion as a woodsman would flee from a hungry bear; or to cling to God with disciplined tenacity, reminding ourselves of who He is, even though our struggle with confusion continues unabated.

**FURTHER STUDY**

Psa. 37:1-9;
Hab. 3:12-19

1. What are we to do when evil people succeed?

2. Why is rejoicing in God not based on circumstances?

In the passage before us today, Habakkuk took the third course. His story begins in great bewilderment and confusion, and the more he questions God, the more confused he becomes. Notice he does not run away from his confusion and pretend it isn't there – he faces it, feels it and presents some pretty tough questions to the Almighty. Notice also that Habakkuk does not become silent until after he has fully entered into and expressed his confusion (2:1). God then reveals Himself to His servant in a way that leads Habakkuk to proclaim a confidence in God that no amount of confusion can shake (3:17-19).

Wouldn't it be wonderful if we could all come through the darkness of confusion with such a treasure? Well, we can. I say again – be open to looking at everything that is happening to you. Don't run too quickly from disturbing events into explanations that are more contrived than real. Contrary to popular Christian opinion, confusion is not bad. Right in the midst of it you can come to know God in a way you never knew Him before.

**Father, help me go into the New Year with a confidence that stands fast even in the midst of confusion. Let the turning point of the year be a turning point also in my spiritual experience. In Jesus' name I pray. Amen.**

# ORDER FORM

## 4 EASY WAYS TO ORDER:

1. Phone in your credit card order: **01252 784710** (Mon-Fri, 9.30am - 5pm)

2. Visit our Online Store at **www.cwr.org.uk/store**

3. Send this form together with your payment to:
   **CWR, Waverley Abbey House, Waverley Lane, Farnham, Surrey GU9 8EP**

4. Visit your local Christian bookshop

or a list of our National Distributors, who supply countries outside the UK, visit www.cwr.org.uk/distributors

## YOUR DETAILS (REQUIRED FOR ORDERS AND DONATIONS)

| | |
|---|---|
| **Name:** | **CWR ID No.** (if known): |
| **Home Address:** | |
| | **Postcode:** |
| **Telephone No.** (for queries): | **Email:** |

## PUBLICATIONS

| TITLE | QTY | PRICE | TOTAL |
|---|---|---|---|
| | | | |
| | | | |
| | | | |
| | | | |
| | | **Total publications** | |

All CWR adult Bible-reading notes are also available in ebook and email subscription format.
Visit **www.cwr.org.uk** for further information.

| | |
|---|---|
| **UK p&p:** up to £24.99 = **£2.99**; £25.00 and over = **FREE** | |
| **Elsewhere p&p:** up to £10 = **£4.95**; £10.01 - £50 = **£6.95**; £50.01 - £99.99 = **£10**; £100 and over = **£30** | |
| Please allow 14 days for delivery                     Total publications and p&p **A** | |

## SUBSCRIPTIONS* (NON DIRECT DEBIT)

| | QTY | PRICE (INCLUDING P&P) | | | TOTAL |
|---|---|---|---|---|---|
| | | UK | Europe | Elsewhere | |
| *Every Day with Jesus* (1yr, 6 issues) | | £15.95 | £19.95 | Please contact nearest National Distributor or CWR direct | |
| Large Print *Every Day with Jesus* (1yr, 6 issues) | | £15.95 | £19.95 | | |
| *Inspiring Women Every Day* (1yr, 6 issues) | | £15.95 | £19.95 | | |
| *Life Every Day* (Jeff Lucas) (1yr, 6 issues) | | £15.95 | £19.95 | | |
| *Cover to Cover Every Day* (1yr, 6 issues) | | £15.95 | £19.95 | | |
| *Mettle*: 14-18s (1yr, 3 issues) | | £14.50 | £16.60 | | |
| *YP's*: 11-15s (1yr, 6 issues) | | £15.95 | £19.95 | | |
| *Topz*: 7-11s (1yr, 6 issues) | | £15.95 | £19.95 | | |
| **Total Subscriptions** (Subscription prices already include postage and packing) **B** | | | | | |

ease circle which bimonthly issue you would like your subscription to commence from:
n/Feb  Mar/Apr  May/Jun  Jul/Aug  Sep/Oct  Nov/Dec

Only use this section for subscriptions paid for by credit/debit card or
cheque. For Direct Debit subscriptions see overleaf.

**CONTINUED OVERLEAF >>**

## PAYMENT DETAILS

☐ I enclose a cheque/PO made payable to CWR for the amount of: **£** _____

☐ Please charge my credit/debit card.

**Cardholder's name** (in BLOCK CAPITALS) _____

Card No. ☐☐☐☐ ☐☐☐☐ ☐☐☐☐ ☐☐☐☐

Expires end ☐☐☐☐        Security Code ☐☐☐

## GIFT TO 25TH ANNIVERSARY THANKS OFFERING   ☐ Please send me an acknowledgement of my gift   **C** ☐

## GIFT AID (YOUR HOME ADDRESS REQUIRED, SEE OVERLEAF)

*giftaid it*

I am a UK taxpayer and want CWR to reclaim the tax on all my donations for the four years prior to this year **and on** all donations I make from the date of this Gift Aid declaration until further notice.*

**Taxpayer's Full Name** (in BLOCK CAPITALS) _____

**Signature** _____ **Date** _____

*I understand I must pay an amount of Income/Capital Gains Tax at least equal to the tax the charity reclaims in the tax year.

**GRAND TOTAL** (Total of A, B, & C) ☐

## SUBSCRIPTIONS BY DIRECT DEBIT (UK BANK ACCOUNT HOLDERS ONLY)

Subscriptions cost £15.95 (except *Mettle*: £14.50) for one year for delivery within the UK. Please tick relevant boxes and fill in the form

☐ *Every Day with Jesus* (1yr, 6 issues)
☐ Large Print *Every Day with Jesus* (1yr, 6 issues)
☐ *Inspiring Women Every Day* (1yr, 6 issues)
☐ *Life Every Day* (Jeff Lucas) (1yr, 6 issues)

☐ *Cover to Cover Every Day* (1yr, 6 issues)
☐ *Mettle*: 14-18s (1yr, 3 issues)
☐ *YP's*: 11-15s (1yr, 6 issues)
☐ *Topz*: 7-11s (1yr, 6 issues)

**Issue to commence**
☐ Jan/Feb ☐ Jul/Aug
☐ Mar/Apr ☐ Sep/Oct
☐ May/Jun ☐ Nov/Dec

## CWR

### Instruction to your Bank or Building Society to pay by Direct Debit

**DIRECT Debit**

Please fill in the form and send to: CWR, Waverley Abbey House, Waverley Lane, Farnham, Surrey GU9 8EP

**Name and full postal address of your Bank or Building Society**

To: The Manager _____ Bank/Building Society

Address _____

Postcode _____

**Name(s) of Account Holder(s)**

_____

**Branch Sort Code**

☐☐ ☐☐ ☐☐

**Bank/Building Society account number**

☐☐☐☐☐☐☐☐

**Originator's Identification Number**

| 4 | 2 | 0 | 4 | 8 | 7 |
|---|---|---|---|---|---|

**Reference**

☐☐☐☐☐☐☐☐☐☐☐☐☐☐

**Instruction to your Bank or Building Society**

Please pay CWR Direct Debits from the account detailed in this Instruction su to the safeguards assured by the Direct Debit Guarantee.

I understand that this Instruction may remain with CWR and, if so, details w passed electronically to my Bank/Building Society.

Signature(s) _____

Date _____

Banks and Building Societies may not accept Direct Debit Instructions for some types of account